Living Hope

*Awakening to Faith, Peace,
and Purpose in Tough Times*

Gerard Long

How can you keep your faith and love for God when first one child dies and then another? As if this wasn't enough, the once beautiful love in his marriage turned to hatred, he died for 30 minutes following a cardiac arrest and he faced sudden financial ruin. In Living Hope, Gerard Long shares what he has learned on his unbelievable journey and how you can awaken faith, peace and purpose during tough times. Read this book and it will make a difference in your life.

> *Ken Blanchard, Co-Author,* The One Minute Manager and Servant Leadership In Action

Gerard and Jeannie Long are a couple whose hearts have been broken. It is difficult to contemplate the agony they have suffered through the tragic loss of two of their children so early in their lives. But their faith and perseverance over the years has been an inspiration. There is much to learn about Christian pilgrimage from those whose wounds are deep.

> *Nicky and Pippa Gumbel, Vicar,* HTB Church, London, and Pioneers of The Alpha Course

When you meet people who live their lives Godward, rather than inward, you are profoundly changed. In Living Hope, you will encounter two such exceptional believers whose insurmountable trials have not made them victims, but victors. And it's why I give a thumbs up to the story of Gerard and Jeannie Long.

> *Joni Eareckson Tada,* Joni and Friends International Disability Center

What a difference it would make in the world if, like Gerard and Jeannie Long, we turned the worst things in our lives into something beautiful to help others! Living Hope is an instructional memoir that will awaken your faith to walk with God through the storms of life. In reading Living Hope, you can discover God's purpose for your life.

> *Roma Downey, Emmy® Nominated Actress, Producer and New York Times Bestselling Author*

The grace and hope flowing through Gerard and Jeannie's story has the potential to have a global impact for good. A true story of redemptive love in the midst of unbelievable suffering and brokenness, it provides comfort and stirs hope and faith for better days ahead.

Samuel Rodriguez, bestselling author and Executive Producer of the 20th Century Fox motion picture Breakthrough

Living Hope provides a unique view of how God's grace works in our lives to prepare us for our calling and purpose. This is a must read for those who long to find their purpose and to fulfill God's call on their lives.

Mark Batterson, Lead Pastor of National Community Church, *New York Times best-selling author of* The Circle Maker

At a time when there is so much suffering and hatred, Gerard and Jeannie's love story shines a message of comfort and hope for better days. It provides comfort to the broken, inspiration and encouragement to the weary and hope to the hopeless.

Philip Anschutz, Businessman, Filmmaker and Philanthropist

Suffering has always been the great challenge to our faith, and Gerard and Jeannie's incredible love story provides a unique lens through which we can see and better understand God in our pain. Providing comfort and hope, this story will stir many to renew their faith in God and their commitment to His plan for their life.

Ted Baehr, Founder of Movieguide.com *and Chairman of the* Christian Film and Television Commission

Inspired by a divine encounter, Gerard and Jeannie are courageously sharing their pain and suffering to give comfort and hope to the broken. Thousands have been helped and inspired by their message, and a movie will bring this unbelievable love story to a bigger global audience.

Jon Burton, Video Game Designer, Writer and Film Director winning five British Academy of Film and Television Arts awards

Rising from the ashes, after the deaths of not one but two of their precious children, Gerard and Jeannie are courageous witnesses to God's amazing grace in the midst of the deepest pain and suffering. Their love story provides a different lens through which to view our unanswered prayers and provides wonderful comfort and hope to anyone who is suffering. On a personal level, Gerard and Jeannie have ministered to me so deeply in my sorrow because of their own pain. They are a profound blessing.

Lani Netter, Film Producer and Influencer, The Shack and Just Mercy Part:1

Gerard and Jeannie's story explores the power of unconditional love in the face of unbelievable loss. It leads us to embrace eternity and to marvel at God's amazing grace.

Steve Fedyski, CEO, Cloudburst Entertainment

I have personally known Gerard for many years. I have been deeply moved by the life of Christ I have found in him even under the most devastating and difficult situations life can throw. His perspective and faith flow from deep places and speak to the power of God to comfort and renew us even in the midst of tragedy and loss.

Scott Chapman, Senior Pastor, The Chapel, Libertyville, IL

After hearing Gerard and Jeannie share their journey of profound and unthinkable suffering, I came away both shaken by the depth of what they have endured and deeply inspired by how they are continuing to hold onto their faith. They have had a significant impact on our church family; God's grace has been clearly evident as they minister to others from their own experiences. I'm grateful that those life insights have been recorded in Living Hope-illustrated by nine seasons that can mark all of our lives. You will be stretched and encouraged as you experience the same grace that has sustained Gerard and Jeannie.

Dr. Jonathan G. Schaeffer, Senior Pastor, Grace Church, Cleveland, OH

I've watched at first hand the unbelievable pain suffered by my good friends Gerard and Jeannie - pain which they have more than survived. Indeed, the radiant joy they have so obviously found in their relationship with God and each other is nothing short of miraculous. I know no one like Gerard who has purposefully turned every potentially devastating circumstance into an opportunity to share the answers that he has found in Jesus with thousands of fellow sufferers. I'm delighted that Gerard has shared the keys to triumphing in disaster with all of us in Living Hope.

Nick West, *Pastoral Lead,* New Life Church, London

Living Hope

Awakening to Faith, Peace,
and Purpose in Tough Times

Gerard Long

Living Hope

Copyright © 2021 by Gerard Long

ISBN: 978-1-7372494-0-5 (Paperback)
ISBN: 978-1-7372494-1-2 (Hardback)
ISBN: 978-1-7372494-2-9 (eBook)
ISBN: 978-1-7372494-3-6 (Audio Book)

Cover design by GSPH
Formatting by Anamaria Stefan

For bulk orders, please email us at: info@livinghopebook.com

To JEANNIE My Beautiful Wife And Best Friend

And Our Three Children
BEN
REBECCA (1982-2014)
ALEXANDER (ALEX) (1987-2005)

CONTENTS

Season Four—Passion with Purpose

Season Five—How to Walk by Faith

Season Six—Harvest Time

Season Seven—"You Will Have Trouble, But..."

Season Eight—New Beginnings

Foreword

For many years, I have had a picture of a wave on my desk!

Working on the cover of *Living Hope*, I reached out to several artists to help with the design. You can imagine, I was curious when one of them proposed a wave. I had to ask, "Why?" The answer was, the wave represented the trouble and suffering we all face in life.

This spoke to me because part of my story is about how we journey through the suffering.

Living by the ocean, I love to swim most days and I know that if I'm not careful, the weight of a wave will crush and drag me under. However, in watching the surfers, I'm inspired as they ride the wave.

Suffering can crush us and drag us under. But, from my own experience, suffering does not have to have the last word.

If you are suffering in any way, I empathize with you. As a brother, a husband, a dad and an uncle, in the space of eight years, I lost two children, my sister, my brother, Jeannie's nephew and my marriage nearly failed.

I want to reassure you that over time, if you let Him, God will comfort and restore you and awaken in you a new purpose.

Jeannie and I have journeyed together in the writing of *Living Hope* and I asked her to write a few words.

"As I write, I'm crying at the mercy of God. Against all odds, Gerard came back to life without any brain damage after being dead for thirty minutes.

I haven't ever read a true story where the writer comes back to life after being dead, other than the Bible of course.

Who better then, to write a book on hope—not just hope—living hope? Someone who has fought for hope in God and fought for me and our son, Ben. My best friend, my husband and now, my courgeous hope warrior.

One universal question is, 'what is hope?' I believe you will find the answer in reading *Living Hope*.

May you find hope as an anchor for your soul. That you can walk without fear, full of hope and light—light that will brighten the days as you introduce the Kingdom of Heaven into your day. Amen and Amen."

Gerard Long

All profits from Living Hope will go to help the suffering via Awakening to God Ministries, a non-profit corporation.

"Hidden in the *heart* of every person is an unquenchable longing to know the purpose of *life*."

Introduction

It was October 26, 2019 and I was dead!

I suffered a cardiac arrest. My heart stopped beating, my breathing ceased, and the medics couldn't revive me. I was clinically dead for more than 30 minutes. And then, miraculously, the paramedics detected a heartbeat.

My beloved Jeannie, my wife of 38 years, had to be half-carried in to see me in the intensive care unit. After all that we had gone through in the previous 15 years, would this be too much for Jeannie's own heart? But, she stayed by my side as she wept and prayed.

Statistics show that only six in every one hundred people who have a cardiac arrest outside a hospital survive. Of those who survive, nine out of ten have irreversible brain damage.

***

As I lay in my bed in the ICU, a question went around and around in my mind: "Why am I still alive?" The answer, I believe, was divinely inspired. God wanted me to share with you the treasures He had given me in the darkness, during a period of unbelievable catastrophic suffering. God brought me back from the dead to tell you about the mystery of His ways through suffering.

This was my inspiration for writing *Living Hope*, and I pray it will give you hope on your journey.

From what I have experienced over the last 60 years—the highs and the lows—I am going to tell you how God prepared me for my purpose and, as shrouded in mystery as it is, I pray my story will give you hope to discover your purpose.

Rewinding the clock on the events leading up to my cardiac arrest, I start my story with my upbringing in the UK. From the beginning, God was preparing me for my purpose. Marrying Jeannie, having three precious children, and enjoying a successful career in banking were all part of the plan. So was our move to New York shortly after 9/11, and our move to Lake Forest, Illinois, in 2003. The first 47 years of my life were wonderfully happy and blessed.

Suddenly, dramatically, my world fell apart. It all started when, out of the blue, my youngest son, Alex, became delusional after smoking marijuana. He broke my heart when he committed suicide.

I can never find the words to describe the pain and suffering. Jeannie was inconsolable. Driven nearly insane by her grief, she went down a very dark path. Her love for me turned to hatred and our marriage hung by a thread. Finally, unable to reconcile how a loving God could have allowed such evil to happen to us, she lost her faith—for a season.

Grieving is hard enough and no parent should have to bury their child–but two children!

Alex's suicide and Rebecca's sudden death was too much for Jeannie's heart to bear. The darkness closed in again. She decided to end her life!

***

In 2015, in obedience to God's calling, we started Awakening to God Ministries to share comfort and hope with the suffering. Moved by God's love, empowered by the Holy Spirit and in loving memory of our children, Rebecca and Alex.

Along the way, a door opened to India and we were privileged to help more than 250,000 of the poorest of the poor by providing clean water wells, mosquito nets, medical aid, and food. It has been a humbling experience to share the love of God with millions of suffering people online, face-to-face, on TV and radio, and through other media. We have been moved to tears by the thousands of messages of appreciation and so grateful for the many testimonies of people that we have helped.

God is close to the brokenhearted and He has been with us in the midst of our sorrow. We know it is only by God's grace and the love, support and prayers of so many that we have journeyed thus far.

My prayer in writing *Living Hope* is that it will help you to hear God's call—His purpose for your life.

Living Hope is organized into what I call "seasons," times in my life that were part of God's plan, preparing me for what was to come.

Season 1—What Is Your Purpose? I've started *Living Hope* by asking what I consider to be the most important questions, questions we often avoid. How you answer these questions will help you open the door to your purpose.

Season 2—Growing from Your Roots. Whether good or bad, God wants to use your upbringing as part of His purpose for your life.

Season 3—What Is in Your Hands? God has blessed you with gifts and abilities.

Season 4—Passion with Purpose. God is love, and He wants you to live a passionate life. A key to discovering your purpose is to recognize the God-given passions of your heart.

Season 5—Learning to Walk by Faith. Fulfilling your purpose requires a walk of faith. In this season I share how faith works and grows through everyday life.

Season 6—A Time to Harvest. In the chapters in this season, I write about a fruitful harvest time on my journey.

Season 7—"You Will Have Trouble, But..." Jesus warned us that we will have trouble. Awakening faith, peace, and purpose in suffering is the key message of *Living Hope*.

Season 8—New Beginnings. In this season I share how God guided Jeannie and me to our new beginnings.

Season 9—The Fight of Faith. The truth is that you have an adversary who is determined to stop you from finding and fulfilling your purpose. Learning to fight the fight of faith is essential to triumph over your adversary and to come into your purpose.

Join the Movement. Imagine what the world would look like if everyone who suffered was comforted. Being restored, they then comforted someone else. My prayer and my vision are for a global tsunami wave of love sweeping around the world.

Faith in Jesus Christ is central to me. So, where I felt it would be helpful, I've explained what my faith means to me and how it impacts my everyday life.

Reading, memorizing, and meditating on scripture is what I do everyday—it's food for my soul. Throughout my story, I have mentioned the Scripture passages that have helped me on my journey. Where I have made a comment based on a scripture, I have given the reference in brackets.

Over 60 years, I've learned many valuable lessons, often through my mistakes. I've highlighted these lessons and my experiences.

I encourage you to use the questions for discussion with a trusted friend or mentor or in a small-group setting.

For confidentiality, most names in my story have been changed.

Season One—What Is Your Purpose?

In the first season of my book, I will share with you the foundation stones of my story—faith, hope and love.

Faith in Christ doesn't guarantee that bad things won't happen to you. However, faith does enable you to see beyond the here and now, and this is what gives you a living hope.

The only way, and it is a mystery, that I was able to journey through catastrophic suffering, is because I had a living hope deep in my soul.

In 1980, I had a powerful encounter with God. My heart, since that day, has been continually stirred by the sweetness of God's love, and this has made all the difference.

God's love and His sovereign power has assured me of His divine plan and purpose for my life. God loves you and has a plan and purpose for your life.

Let me begin by sharing the miracle of my recovery from the cardiac arrest.

1.

Dead for 30 Minutes

I have no recollection of what I'm about to tell you. I've pieced it together from Jeannie and my friends.

It was October 26, 2019. I had set my alarm for 12:30 am, dressed as quietly as I could and I kissed Jeannie good bye. She said, "I love you. Enjoy the rugby with the boys." I was so pleased that my friends had invited me to join them to watch the game in their home. It was going to be broadcast live from Tokyo at 1:00 am in the morning.

Just as I was leaving, I turned and said to Jeannie, "We are in God's hands." The words seemed to strangely hang in the air, and Jeannie replied, "Yes, we are always in God's hands."

England had reached the semi-final of the Rugby World Cup. Their next opponents were the All Blacks, the reigning world champions and the number one team in the world. It was going to be a huge game and I had an adrenalin rush just thinking about it.

My friend Deryck greeted me, with his sons Joel and Josiah, and our good friend, Adam. It was just before kick-off and I could feel the tremendous buzz of anticipation. It was going to be a fantastic match.

England got off to a great start, and two minutes after kickoff, they scored a tremendous try. My friends looked over and to their surprise,

I was slumped in my chair with no reaction to England's try (which is unheard of for me!). It appeared as though I was having a seizure. In fact, I was having a cardiac arrest. My heart stopped. My breathing stopped. No oxygen was getting to my brain or other vital organs.

Deryck prayed, called 911 and reported I was having a seizure, which is not the top priority. I'm beyond grateful that Josiah identified that I was actually having a cardiac arrest. Suddenly, that changed everything. Deryck called 911 again and told them it was a cardiac arrest. I was now top priority. Adam and Joel quickly pulled me to the floor. Adam sensed God telling him to start CPR, specifically to do 30 pumps on my chest, followed by two mouth-to-mouth breaths.

Deryck woke his wife Rozie, a former nurse. Unable to find a pulse or evidence of breathing, Rozie said, "I'm very sorry, he's gone."

It's a mystery why Joel and Adam refused to accept that death would have the last word. They entered into a fight for my life. Joel began to shout for me to come back, while Adam threw up a desperate prayer.

"Lord, if You bring Gerard back, I will do anything You want."

After ten minutes of CPR, there was still no pulse. Exhausted, Adam was relieved when the first responders arrived.

"Keep up the chest pumps!" one of them shouted, while they prepared their equipment.

The emergency team took over from Adam, and for the next twenty minutes, they worked to bring me back to life.

After several electric shocks to my heart, the paramedics were unable to revive me, Adam and Joel refused to give up the fight and pleaded for one more electric shock.

Their prayers were answered when the miraculous happened. My heart started beating!

Immediately, they rushed me to the UCLA emergency room in Santa Monica, where they worked for hours to bring me fully back to life. My friends followed the ambulance to the hospital and prayed for me through the night. My good friend Jonathan and his wife Hannah, just happened to be visiting Malibu and, even though she was eight months pregnant, they joined the others in praying for me.

"How do we tell Jeannie?" my friends asked, knowing that we had already journeyed through the passing of our son Alex and, eight years later, our daughter Rebecca.

At 4 am, Jeannie awoke with a jolt. Seeing that I still wasn't home, she blocked out the voices of fear. But, when she opened up her text messages, she read this,

"Gerard has had an accident."

"He's in hospital, but the good news is, he's stable."

In shock, Jeannie prayed as she waited for Deryck and Rozie to drive her to the hospital. On the way, they gently prayed and prepared her for what she was about to face.

At the hospital, Jonathan was waiting outside to meet Jeannie. He and Rozie helped Jeannie to the ICU waiting room, where she was greeted, hugged and prayed for by Hannah, Joel, Adam and Josiah.

Rozie held Jeannie's hand as they walked into the ICU. When she saw me unconscious, with tubes and wires all over me, the blood drained from her face, and she had to be helped to a chair.

Before leaving home, Jeannie had grabbed some of my scripture cards, which I use to memorize verses. With Rozie supporting her, Jeannie stood beside me and spoke over me some of my favorite Scriptures. One of them was,

I will sing of the LORD's great love forever; with my mouth I will make your faithfulness known through all generations.

Psalm 89:1

Jeannie wanted to stay with me, but because I was in an induced 24 hour coma, the medical staff persuaded her to go home and get some rest.

After Deryck and Rozie dropped her off at home, Jeannie fell to the floor and through her tears she cried out, "Lord, I need a miracle."

Not long after, the ICU doctor called Jeannie.

"Please come back to the hospital as soon as you can," he said. "This is very unusual. We normally have to wake patients from an induced coma, but he's woken up on his own and is trying to pull out his wires and get out of bed. Please get here as soon as you can."

It was an answer to Jeannie's prayer that I was awake, but when she arrived at the ICU, she was surprised to find me tied to my bed. She later told me that I seemed to want to get out of the hospital to finish an assignment. I was muttering something about having to "get on and finish the work."

I'd been clinically dead for at least 30 minutes. A surgeon had inserted two stents in my left coronary artery, which was 100 percent blocked.

When I later discovered that artery is called the "widow-maker," I told Jeannie. She burst into tears and thanked God for His mercy.

As well as keeping my heart beating, the medics were particularly concerned about the effect on my brain, kidneys, and other vital organs, after being deprived of oxygen for so long. The prayers of Jeannie and my friends had been answered. I had defied all the odds by surviving, but judging by the following statistics, it was not looking good for my brain and other vital organs.

Every year in the U.S., approximately 395,000 cases of cardiac arrest occur outside of a hospital setting, in which less than six percent survive. 90 percent of those who survive have some sort of brain damage, according to the National Academy of Sciences.

The time came for me to have an MRI on my brain. Adam joined Jeannie and together they desperately prayed that I would have no brain damage.

Their prayers were answered when, suddenly, a doctor burst through the doors, saying, "It's a miracle, it's a miracle, he doesn't have any brain damage!"

The first responders, ICU nurses and doctors, said my survival was a miracle.

The main question I'm asked is, "What did you see when you were dead?"

I honestly can't remember. But what I do know, is that I'm now alive after my unexpected and unexplained death! In His mercy and grace, God has given me more time on earth because my race is not yet finished. I have something to share. This is why I wrote *Living Hope.*

I pray from the depths of my now beating heart that my story will encourage and inspire you on your journey.

2.

Faith - What Is It?

Now faith is the substance of things hoped for, the evidence of things not seen.

Hebrews 11:1

In my encounter with God in 1980, I put my faith in Jesus Christ. In believing in Christ, God opened my spiritual eyes through the Holy Spirit, who came to live in me.

Through the gift of faith, I understood things about God I had never seen before. My life changed dramatically and I began a new journey of adventure, pursuing God and His purpose for me.

On my journey, my faith grew as I trusted in God's promises. It opened up a whole other world. A spiritual dimension that I can't see with my natural eyes. But, through my eyes of faith, I can see the supernatural in the natural.

In viewing my life through the eyes of faith, I can see that God is working His plan and purpose in me. My deep faith has enabled me to overcome and triumph, even in catastrophic suffering.

The faith, love, and joy in my heart flow from a living hope that this life is just the beginning of a never ending story.

The Bible teaches that the things we see with our natural eyes are temporary, but the things that are unseen are eternal (2 Corinthians 4:18).

Life is like a mountain. Sometimes the climb is easy and enjoyable but then a storm comes out of nowhere and the going is tough, and it's a struggle. During the last 16 years, I've had a struggle and, at times, I have had to really fight to hold to my faith.

By God's grace, I am still on my journey, my race that is set before me, and I'm humbled in how He is using the worst things in my life to help others.

> *I have learned that:*
>
> *- it takes courage to live by faith, to say to God, "not my will, but yours be done";*
>
> *- things that might be considered coincidences are actually God touching my life; and*
>
> *- there is another dimension, a spiritual dimension, that can't be seen with my natural eyes.*

3.

Living Hope

At the time of this writing, the world is gripped by the COVID-19 pandemic, which has changed everyone's life. The level of suffering and hopelessness is unprecedented.

Life is fragile and it can be hard, and sometimes it's a struggle to have hope. These are the times to look within yourself and be honest with God, and others, about your struggles.

I have learned that in my darkest times I can grow closer to God, than at any other time. Being totally honest with God, my faith has grown and hope has sprung up from deep within.

When I open myself up to God, I open a door in my heart to His love. The Holy Spirit comforts me and empowers me with Jesus' life.

During His time on earth, Jesus experienced great suffering for all of us. Therefore, He is able to empathize with my suffering and He knows exactly what I need for each new day. I am comforted in the knowledge that when I suffer, He suffers with me.

There have been times in my life, when great pain and discouragement have nearly extinguished the light of hope in my soul. But walking through the flames of suffering, I have learned that the God of all hope is always with me and His great love for me remains constant.

This makes all the difference as I face the challenge of each new day.

My faith and the knowledge of God's love for me, have enabled me to see that He is working through my suffering, to prepare me for my purpose. Seeing a divine purpose for my suffering has given me hope. I trust Him with my life and my future.

Because of Jesus' resurrection from the dead, He has put eternity within our hearts, and He will make all things beautiful in His time. The greatest things are yet to come!

I have hope—but not just any hope, I have *living hope*.

4.

Love - God Has a Plan for You

Are we here by accident, living in time and space without any bigger purpose or meaning?

Or

Is there a God who has a purpose and plan for our lives?

One cold winter's afternoon in the UK, I had an interesting conversation with a friend over a nice cup of tea and a McVities chocolate biscuit. He was an atheist and as far as he was concerned, there is no God.

"According to what you believe, where have we all come from?", I asked him.

Without hesitation, he mentioned the theory of evolution.

"At a point in time, there was a big bang," he said. "Since then, we have been evolving on a random basis, together with the survival of the fittest."

We've all heard this view many times before. I asked him another question.

"Do you believe there is any meaning or purpose for our lives?"

"Oh, no," he said. "We are a function of chance. Everything is random, and whatever happens in our lives is down to fate. We have come from nowhere, and when we die, that is it. Nothing."

Another time, after preaching at a church, I had a conversation with a young man over a coffee. He thanked me for the message I shared but went on to say that he didn't believe God had a plan for his life.

"I'm interested to hear your views on God's role in our lives," I said.

"I have no problem in believing there is a God or a force that is greater than us," he said. "But whatever is out there, has no interest in us on a personal level, and there is certainly no divine plan for our lives."

"Where do you think we have come from?" I asked.

After acknowledging that God or another force started things off, he said, "But we have evolved randomly in line with the theory of evolution." He continued, "As far as I'm concerned, I have to make my own destiny."

I respect the views of both my friend in the UK, and the young man.

Humbly, I will share with you what I believe.

I believe God exists outside of time, space, and matter. He exists in another dimension. He created the universe and everything in it. He holds every atom together by His power (Hebrews 1:3, Romans 11:36, Acts 17:28). He is over all things, and He is working everything out for His eternal plan and purpose.

It's breathtaking to me, and fills my heart with joy and wonder, that God is love and He created us for a relationship with Him. He wants us to know and understand Him (Jeremiah 9:23-24, Philippians 3:10). In His perfect love, God gave us the freedom to choose or to reject Him. It's heartbreaking to know that humankind rebelled against God and we decided to go our own way. Through Jesus Christ, God made a way for everyone to come back into a relationship with Him.

In the relationship, God has an eternal purpose and plan for each one of us. He has promised to equip us with everything we need to complete the plan and to guide us through life and along the path prepared for us.

I have learned to share Christ's love by listening, respecting and asking others for their view.

5.

What Is Your Purpose?

Life is an exploration into the unknown. You can choose many roads, but only one of them has been planned by God.

Following God's road will involve a decision similar to the one found in the words in Robert Frost's poem "The Road Not Taken":

Two roads diverged in a wood, and I—
I took the one less traveled by,
And that has made all the difference.

To me, the poem reflects the incredible free will God has given us to choose the road we are going to take.

God does have a plan and purpose for your life, a special road for you to walk down. But, you may decide to go a different way, to choose your own road.

Jesus showed us how to walk down the road His Father had planned for Him. He never lived for His own will, only for the will of His Father. Jesus said,

For I have come down from heaven not to do my will but to do the
will of him who sent me.

John 6:38

Season
Two—Growing from Your Roots

To discover God's purpose for your life, you should start by understanding your roots.

Over the next few pages, I'm going to tell you about my family and spiritual roots. As you read, please think about your family and spiritual roots and consider how God may be working through them to point you to your purpose. What sort of relationship did you have with your parents and your siblings? Were there any experiences in your childhood that had a significant impact on your life, for good or for bad?

As they say, you can choose your friends, but you can't choose your family. Some people are born into a wonderful family. They are loved and cared for by their parents and siblings and have a supportive extended family. Others are born into dysfunctional families. Maybe they were abused growing up, and their childhood memories are mainly unhappy and bathed in fear and insecurity.

Others are born into a loving family but in a geographic area of extreme poverty, where life hangs by a thread and the pain of losing a loved one is ever-present. Still others are born into both a dysfunctional family *and* extreme poverty.

And of course, some people's upbringing involves more than one of the above scenarios.

The fact is, we live in a broken world, where there is awful suffering and horrible experiences. Your family and the early years of your life are formative in who you are.

The good news is that God is bigger than your circumstances and experiences, and His love and power can reach you wherever you were born and whatever roots you have. If you let Him, God has a way of turning the bad things in your life into something good.

I have met men and women who have turned what Satan intended for evil into good, to help and encourage others. I'm inspired by their stories, and I pray they will encourage you too.

As a child, Joyce Meyer was raped more than a hundred times by her father, and her mother knew what was going on. Today, she is one of the most influential women speakers in America and across the world. She has encouraged, inspired, and given hope to millions of people through her books, television and radio shows and appearances, and at conferences. She has also given generously to help the poor. Instead of becoming bitter over the pain and suffering her family caused, she discovered and participated in her God-given purpose. She allowed God to turn what Satan intended for evil into something good to help millions of people.

Nick Vujicic is a remarkable man who was born without any limbs. As a boy, he considered suicide by drowning in his bath. Thinking about the pain it would cause his mom, he decided not to carry out his plan. Accepting God's call on his life, Nick came into his purpose and started a ministry called Life Without Limbs. Nick has inspired millions of people all around the world to be grateful and to consider how they can help others. Nick has every reason to be bitter and resentful, but instead, he has found his purpose in helping others.

As a 17-year-old, Joni Eareckson Tada was paralyzed from the shoulders down when she dove into the Chesapeake Bay in Maryland but miscalculated the depth of the water. Enduring significant pain and suffering, including cancer, bouts of depression and suicidal thoughts, and a COVID-19 diagnosis, Joni has inspired and encouraged millions of people with more than forty books, a film, television and radio appearances, several musical albums, and generous giving to the disabled community. Joni could easily have become angry and bitter, but instead, she allowed God to use her pain to help others.

Jim Daly was abandoned by his alcoholic father at age five and was orphaned by his mother's death from cancer when he was nine. He then went through the foster home system and lived on his own as a high school senior. Jim now heads Focus on the Family, one of the most influential Christian communication ministries in the world. Jim has said that the pain and suffering he experienced growing up prepared him for his work in Focus on the Family.

Because of the 1994 Rwandan genocide, a man named Frank was an orphan living on the streets. Jeannie and I met Frank as our taxi driver in Chicago in 2018. He told us his story, and when he said he wanted to start an orphanage in Rwanda, we knew Frank had a warrior heart. He wanted God to turn the evil that had happened to him into something good to help others. We are now partnering with Frank in running an orphanage in Rwanda.

We have a choice in how we respond to our family upbringing and experiences.

I pray you will have the courage to fully embrace your family roots

I pray that this season of my story will help you to understand your own roots and to grow in a way that awakens you to faith, peace, and purpose.

6.

My Parents

My mom met my dad when she was 14 years old, and from that first meeting, she knew he was the one she wanted to marry. A few years later, my father proposed, and they were married when she was 19 and he was 22.

I had a happy upbringing. I was the youngest of four children, and my home was full of love.

My parents were Christians. What I most remember is how they loved each other, my siblings, and me. They were hospitable, and I remember meeting many interesting people who visited our home.

My dad was the most loving and humble man I have ever known. I don't ever remember hearing him say anything bad about anyone. When he greeted you, he would tuck his head into your neck and give you an almighty hug.

My dad was a gifted speaker and was often invited to preach at some of the small village chapels that were dotted across the South Downs, the green rolling hills in the south of England. I loved it when I could go with him.

My dad owned a retail business selling boating, skiing, and camping goods. He worked hard and although he had some struggles with his business, he never complained. Sensing a fresh call from God, he sold his business after 27 years and served as the pastor of Ledbury Baptist church in Wiltshire, England

My mom's love for the Lord Jesus was a great example to me and everyone who met her. I have memories of walking into her bedroom and finding her on her knees praying. She didn't look up, and I would quietly back out of the room, not wanting to disturb her time with God.

My mom was a rock in our family and was highly respected by all who knew her. I remember her strength and her great character in the way she brought me and my siblings up.

In 1995, my dad suddenly died of a heart attack. He was only 67 years old. It was a huge shock for my mom and all the family, and it was my first experience of grief. It makes my survival from the cardiac arrest all the more remarkable, because my grandfather also died of a heart attack.

> *I have learned that:*
>
> *- the most effective way parents can tell their children about God's love is by loving each other;*
>
> *- it is better to give than to receive, and that to serve and contribute to the community brings great joy.*

How about you? What are the main things you remember about your parents? What would you say were their strongest qualities?

7.

My Siblings

My three siblings and I were born within five and a half years of each other.

My older sister was named Jacqueline but we called her "Jax." She had green eyes and curly hair and she loved horses. Over the summer holidays, she would take me and my brothers on wild adventures riding the horses in the fields behind our house. Sometimes we would ride horses in the South Downs and I was often the stunt person for her latest trick. I remember she wanted to find out if one particular horse could jump over fences, and I volunteered to find out! Yes, the horse could jump over the fence, but when it landed, I fell off. Because I never seemed to hurt myself and always bounced back, I was nicknamed the rubber boy.

Kim is my eldest brother, and I looked up to him. He loved sports and was a great engineer in our back garden. Following his leadership, we tied ropes high into the trees and came flying down on pulleys. We dug tunnels and caves deep into the ground and played soccer and rugby late into the evenings. Kim has been a good brother to me, and when I first left home we had great fun sharing a small apartment.

William, whom we called Will, was my middle brother, and we competed at almost everything. The first back to the car, the most swims in the sea (even when it was freezing cold), and to win every game we competed in. My mom once came home to find Will and me in a big fight over a board game, with his blood all over the place from my punch to his nose—even though he was two years older than me. I remember having great fun with Will and his friends on adventures in the neighborhood.

8.

Happy Memories

We lived in a comfortable five-bedroom house in a small village on the south coast of England. My bedroom window overlooked a field and I could hear the waves and smell the salty sea air. In the springtime the beautiful cherry blossom trees in our garden came alive with color and fragrance, along with the snowdrops, crocuses, bluebells, and daffodils that broke through the lush green grass. It's hard to beat the English springtime.

We spent long summer days at the beach, and on Sunday afternoons we went for family walks in the countryside. We lived near Chichester, an old Roman city where you can still see parts of the original Roman wall. A few miles away in Fishbourne is the remains of a Roman palace, which is the largest residential Roman building in Britain. One of our favorite villages, Bosham, is an old, picturesque, smuggler's village on the Chichester estuary. Some parts of Bosham Church are more than a thousand years old! My grandparents owned a small cottage in Bosham overlooking the water, and we would often sail and swim in the estuary with our cousins.

We didn't have a television until I was 10 years old, and in those days, there were no computer games or internet. We were usually outside playing sports (mainly soccer) or going on another adventure. Those were great times, and we had tremendous fun. We climbed onto and into old, deserted houses, we rode bareback on horses that seemed to be wild, and we tied cotton thread to door knockers and watched in peals of laughter as the occupants tried to figure out who kept knocking at their front door.

The greatest fun for me was to be chased. I was a fast runner, so I could usually get away, unless my laughter weakened me so much that I couldn't run. These were days of great adventure, laughter, long summer evenings playing on the lawn, the smell of freshly cut grass and going to the beach or the South Downs. Life was great.

In England, it was a tradition to have a delicious Sunday roast. Sometimes I found myself thinking about the Sunday roast during the pastor's sermon, as I looked forward to what was to come. I remember my father sharpening his carving knife and serving us slices of delicious roast beef, together with roast potatoes, two vegetables like peas and carrots, and a Yorkshire pudding. Yorkshire pudding, an English tradition, consists of eggs, milk, and flour. It rises in the oven into the shape of a bowl. I loved the taste of the Yorkshire pudding, especially when I poured gravy into it to soften it.

My competitive nature would often get me into trouble. At junior school we played a game called "wall to wall," where you had to run between the walls without being tagged. The last player tagged was the winner. On three occasions, I was running so fast and was so intent on not being caught that I couldn't stop and I split my head open on the wall (that could explain a lot!). After stitching me up for the third time, the doctors warned me that my skin was too thin to take another knock.

I'm grateful for my happy and privileged childhood, knowing that for many people, their early years were difficult. We go through different seasons in our lives, and God uses the good and the bad to weave a story into our lives as part of His eternal plan and purpose for us.

Your family, your upbringing, and your experiences have contributed to who you are. Even if you have painful memories, I encourage you to consider how they influence you today. God's ways are so much higher than our ways, and He may be wanting to use what you consider to be a weakness or a painful memory as something powerful to help others.

9.

My Spiritual Roots

I am thankful for my spiritual roots. My family traces its lineage to the Huguenots—a group of 16th and 17th-century Christians who fled France to save their lives during a time of persecution because they refused to renounce their faith. Many persecuted Huguenots settled in England.

Generations later, looking for a closer walk with God, they formed a denomination called the Brethren, with leaders such as George Müller and John Darby, who were both great men of faith.

My spiritual eyes were opened in my childhood, through the influence of my parents and my three siblings. My mom was a great storyteller who made the Bible come alive to me through our bedtime stories. In the mornings, my dad would do a Bible reading with a lesson over breakfast.

When I was young, my parents took me to some nondenominational meetings, where I first experienced God's presence. I remember sitting in church listening to the most beautiful singing. Although I was young, I felt deeply moved inside. As I looked around the room, I was fascinated to see people with their arms raised and their smiling faces looking up. They seemed to love God and I learned that day what it meant to praise and worship Him.

I have great memories of attending Christian youth clubs and camps after that "otherworldly" experience. One of my fondest memories is of going to the Christian Special Seaside Mission (CSSM) during the summer holidays. I still remember the excitement of waking up early in the morning and waiting for the camper van to pick up me and my siblings, together with some friends and an orphan who were staying with us. We would laugh and sing songs as we traveled across town for a morning Bible study. I found it to be such fun studying God's Word; I loved learning the memory verse. At any time during the day, one of the young leaders would stop me and ask, "Psst, what's the password?" This was code for, "Tell me your memory verse."

As the day went on, we would have what we called tide fights—teams would build the strongest sand castles they could, and as the tide came in, the last one standing won. After lunch, we piled back into the camper van and went to the countryside for more games. CSSM was a fantastic week of fun and games, while I was also learning Bible stories, memorizing scripture, and making new friends. All these years later, I still sing some of the CSSM songs. A few years ago, Jeannie and I were delighted to accept an invitation by our friend Lani to her father's 103rd birthday party. Lani asked me to come to the front to lead us all in a song. Yes, you guessed it, I chose a song I had learned from CSSM:

> *Joy is the flag flown high from the castle of my heart,*
> *from the castle of my heart, from the castle of my heart;*
> *Joy is the flag flown high from the castle of my heart,*
> *When the King is in residence there.*
>
> *So let it fly in the sky and let the whole world know,*
> *let the whole world know, let the whole world know;*
> *So let it fly in the sky let the whole world know,*
> *that the King is in residence there!*

10.

My Calling

The Bible teaches that God calls us to the work He has planned for us to do. We are all called to love God and others and to tell people about Him. And, God has called each one of us to a specific work such as nursing, banking, pastoring in a church, etc.

> *I have learned that God reveals His plan for me as I truly seek Him.*

God wants us to be faithful to our calling. We should never compare ourselves to others, because we each have a unique calling, and God gives us the resources and abilities to complete the work.

"Long may he serve his God!" To her own surprise, those were the words my mom prophesied over me as I came into the world. You could say that this was an early calling for me.

For as long as I can remember, I've always believed in God, and I've often been aware of His presence. But, my faith has been severely tested in the furnace of suffering.

11.

The Anchor for My Faith

We all have our highs and our lows, and what has made *all* the difference for me is not letting go of what I believe in when the darkness closes in. As I write, because of the COVID-19 pandemic, many people are in a low season and have lost all hope. I want to tell you about the anchor that I have discovered for my faith.

When Satan, the enemy of our soul, tempts us with his whispers of doubt, I believe it takes great courage to resist him, especially when experiencing a furnace of suffering. For me, three overwhelming pieces of evidence anchor my faith in God.

First, I stand in awe and wonder of creation. It is too mind-blowing and too beautiful to have happened by chance. How incredible that every snowflake is unique! Every flower has a different shape, color, and fragrance. It's marvelous that there should be such a fantastic variety of animals. How remarkable that a tiny bird can produce such a perfect tune with such volume! How wonderful that a tiny acorn, planted in the right environment, will produce a mighty oak tree! How striking that every sky has a different color. How staggering that earth has the exact combination of oxygen, nitrogen, carbon dioxide, and other gases that enable us to live here. How mind-boggling it is that the sun is at the exact distance from earth to support life and not destroy it. What about the human body? There are trillions of cells in the human body, and each has millions of interrelated parts. And how lovely is romance and the uniqueness of families and the gift of a new baby!

I believe God created the universe and everything in it. However, as marvelous as creation is, what we see today is only its fallen state, because it has been spoiled by our sin and rebellion against God.

The second reason I believe in God is because of Jesus Christ. I believe that God actually visited our planet some two thousand years ago, in the person of Jesus Christ. The evidence is overwhelming—God actually walked among us on this planet.

My faith is based on God's promises in Jesus Christ, as recorded in the Bible. Roman and Jewish historians have written about Jesus. In fact, no one doubts that Jesus walked on this earth and that He was fully man. What is questioned is whether He was and is fully God. As a young boy, I believed He was, and I now have evidence to support my faith.

As C.S. Lewis puts it, there are only three possible explanations for Jesus' claim to be God: He was evil and wanted to deceive people, or He was crazy, or He truly was the Son of God. Lewis provided five measures to assess who Jesus is. For each one, we ask the question that most fits the evidence of Jesus, as follows:

His teaching. Although we have progressed in areas such as science and technology, in the last two thousand years no one has ever improved on Jesus' teaching on our moral behavior. It is the basis for legal systems around the world. Does this fit with Jesus being evil, crazy, or God?

His character. Jesus was loved by people who had no political or religious power. In particular, He was loved by outcasts and children. Children can usually tell if someone is a bit odd. Does this fit with Jesus being evil, crazy, or God?

Prophecy. Jesus fulfilled more than three hundred Old Testament prophecies—written hundreds of years before His birth. Some people say Jesus learned the prophecies and sought to fulfill them during His life, but it's hard to bring about where you are going to be born or how you will be killed and where you are going to be buried! Does this fit with Jesus being evil, crazy, or God?

His miracles. These were recorded by historians at the time, in addition to being in the Bible. He raised the dead to life, He walked on water, He calmed the wind and the waves. But only God is above created things and the natural laws of this world. Does this fit with Jesus being evil, crazy, or God?

His resurrection from the dead. Some people suggest that He didn't die, but the evidence doesn't support this. Jesus endured a Roman flogging; many prisoners would die from this alone. He was violently beaten and was so disfigured that He was unrecognizable. He clearly died and was later seen alive. Does this fit with Jesus being evil, crazy, or God?

As to that final point, when they inspected Jesus—they wanted to complete the crucifixion before the start of the Passover—they found that He was already dead. If He hadn't been dead, they would have broken His legs. That would have caused suffocation, because He couldn't have pushed up with His legs to get air into His lungs.

A guard thrust his spear into Jesus' side, and blood and water gushed out, which is medical evidence of death.

Some suggest that He didn't rise from the dead, but the evidence doesn't support this. Shortly before Jesus' crucifixion, His disciples fled from Him, and terrified, they locked themselves in an upper room.

But, shortly after His death they became very bold, and willing to die, they turned the world upside down with their preaching about Jesus. It's highly unlikely they would have changed so dramatically if they knew Jesus was permanently dead and their hopes and prayers had died with Him. Later, they were martyred. Would they have done this if they knew Jesus was dead and had not been resurrected?

The historic evidence records that Jesus rose from the dead, proving His defeat and triumph over death itself. Earlier He had claimed that He was the resurrection and the life. He appeared to more than five hundred people over a six-week period (1 Corinthians 15:6).

As a young boy, I didn't know all of the evidence for Jesus being God, but I knew enough to put my trust and hope in Him.

The third reason I believe in Jesus Christ is because I saw my parents living out their Christian faith every day in our home. Either my parents, and the two billion or so other Christians, imagined things, or worse, I was being deceived. Or it was true. I believed it was true.

Creation, Jesus Christ, and the number of Christ-followers today, and through the ages, anchor my faith in God. The first two are recorded in the Bible, along with God's instructions and promises to humankind.

I didn't have all this worked out as a young boy, but I wanted to ask Jesus into my life.

Although I was only five years old, I remember kneeling with my big sister Jax beside her bed and saying a simple prayer.

"Jesus, thank You for dying on the cross for me. Please forgive me of my sin and please come and live in my heart. Thank You for being my Good Shepherd, and please guide me through the rest of my life. Amen."

My prayer was genuine, and I believe, as scripture says, God answered it by transferring me into His kingdom and giving me a new heart—I was born again by the Spirit of God!

> *For he has rescued us from the kingdom of darkness and transferred us into the Kingdom of his dear Son, who purchased our freedom and forgave our sins.*
>
> **Colossians 1:13-14 NLT**

> *I have learned that what we believe in provides a lens through which we view our lives and the world in which we live.*

When our daughter Rebecca was a little girl, she loved ladybugs. After a visit to an optician, she had to wear glasses. It was so sweet when she said to me, "Daddy, all the ladybugs have little black dots."

> *I have learned that if the lens through which I view life is distorted, how I view myself, others, and the world in which I live will be incomplete and incorrect.*

How about you, what do you believe? What have you put your hope and faith in? Whatever or whomever your faith is in will be foundational to how you live out your life. Even an atheist has faith in the belief that there is no God and no life after death.

Consider your beliefs and your worldview, and how they influence how you live. Start with your family and write down five ways in which your faith and worldview influence your relationships.

Season Three—What Is in Your Hands?

Our gifts and abilities help guide us to our purpose. I believe these are things God has placed in our hands for our own good and to help others.

I learned from watching my parents and from listening to what they taught me from the Bible. I learned what it means to love people. I remember my parents inviting to our home a troubled teenager from a British charity founded to care for vulnerable children. My siblings and I felt a bit put out by the young man, but it taught me a valuable lesson about practical love.

I saw that it is better to give than to receive, to be kind and not to be jealous of what others have. To be grateful for whatever God has given me.

I saw how my parents respected everyone, whatever their background or the color of their skin, and how every person was welcome in our home. My parents were often thinking of others and how they could help them.

Despite many challenges, my parents maintained a positive attitude, and they never judged or bore a grudge against anyone. Forgiveness seemed to flow like a river in our home. I was taught the importance of telling the truth and the responsibility I had to help and protect the weak and the vulnerable.

I remember how hard my parents worked and how patient they were with my siblings and me, even though our rebellious behavior must have been heartbreaking for them. They persevered and never gave up on us. My parents also impressed upon me the importance of keeping away from the occult and to be aware of Satan's schemes to ensnare people.

If I had applied all of the lessons I learned from my parents, I would have been a poster child for Christianity.

Unfortunately, my selfishness and natural tendency to do wrong won out far too often, and I was regularly getting into trouble at home and at school.

The boys at school looked up to me and followed me as a leader, but time and again I led them in the wrong direction. I was a fighter, and I still remember the sinking feeling in my stomach when, once again, I was sent to the headmaster's office. One time he even bent me over his knee and gave me the cane—a British form of corporal punishment. Teachers were allowed to do that in my day.

To keep me from going completely off the rails, my parents decided to send me to a military school.

But I had received the seeds for godly and wise living, and my parents faithfully prayed that they would eventually bear fruit in my life. They clung to this Scripture:

Train up a child in the way he should go, and when he is old he will not depart from it.

Proverbs 22:6

12.

Military School

Suddenly, at 11 years old, I found myself alone, away from my loving family and friends, my dog named Shandy, and everything that had been so comfortable and familiar to me. For the next five years, I discovered a whole other level of what discipline is all about.

My parents sent me away to the Gordon Boys' School, a tough military boarding school founded in memory of General Charles George Gordon, a British military hero who was killed in an uprising in 1885 in Khartoum, Sudan. The school, located thirty miles south of London, had a student body that was mainly made up of boys aged 11 to 16, from military families serving overseas.

Each and every day was intense and disciplined, but the competitive ethos of the school suited my personality. My day started at 7 a.m. with a bugle call for the boys to get up, stand in line for the washroom, dress in our gray school uniform, and be ready for another bugle call at 7:20 a.m. to march to the "cook house," where we had our meals. We would fall in outside our barracks into a three-line squad formation and march to the cook house, whatever the weather—rain, sleet, or snow.

Breakfast consisted of a fried egg, a piece of fried bread, fried tomatoes and baked beans, a bowl of cereal, bread and jam, and a cup of tea. The boys would barter for different parts of the meal, with fried bread and the cereal being the most popular. After breakfast we had about thirty minutes to clean the barracks, including the restrooms, before another bugle call to attend school. On Mondays, the whole school had assembly, which included reports on the school athletic matches over the weekend.

Morning school was followed by another bugle call to the cook house for lunch. We would again fall in and march to have our meal.

After lunch, we would either have sports followed by afternoon school, or vice versa. Dinnertime was the same—bugle, fall in, march, and eat. After dinner, we would have a short break before a bugle call to start homework, between 7 p.m. and 8:15 p.m. This was followed by more household chores, getting ready for bed, and as you might have guessed, a final bugle call for lights out at 9:30 p.m.

During Saturday morning school, our barracks were inspected, so the previous Friday night and early Saturday, there was frantic activity to lay out our kit and make sure everything was spick and span. After school we had lunch, followed by sports. If you didn't have a match you could get a pass to be out for the afternoon. On Saturday evening, I loved the treat of watching a movie in the school hall with a pocket full of candy.

Sunday morning we had a church parade. For this, we wore our Gordon Tartan pants, a wool jacket, and a beret. We spent some time pressing the pants, spit-polishing our shoes, and shining the badge on our beret. After chapel we marched passed the headmaster before being allowed to go out for the afternoon with parents or friends. On Sunday afternoon, we would often have inter-house sports competitions.

The student body was divided into four houses, and each house was named after different stages in General Gordon's life.

Woolwich, the junior house, was where Gordon was born and grew up; Gravesend, where Gordon received military training; China, where he received a yellow jacket for serving the emperor; and Khartoum, where he fought and died for queen and country.

We competed in everything you can imagine—every sport, with soccer, rugby, and cross-country being the most intense. We also competed in house-cleaning, academic points, marching, and activities such as chess. As you can imagine, the boys got up to all sorts of mischief, and we had lots of fun, including pillow fights and inter-house raids.

The boys ran the houses based on military ranking. At the top was a regimental sergeant major, known as the head boy, followed by four house sergeants (one for each house), corporals and lance corporals (in charge of the dormitories in the house). This worked well. However, occasionally there was bullying, and at its very worst, the older boys would abuse the younger boys. I did experience some bullying in my first two years, but I'm grateful that I was kept safe from any abuse. I believe this was because of my parents' prayers.

I believe God directed my parents to send me to the military school. It was part of my training and preparation for what God had planned for later in my life.

The Apostle Paul often compares the Christian walk with that of a soldier (2 Timothy 2:3-4 and Ephesians 6:11-18). Although it was very hard at times, my experience at Gordon's taught me many valuable lessons. Later, these became key foundation stones in my walk with Christ.

> *I have learned how important discipline is, and in particular, self-discipline.*

Self-discipline is the decision to do what is right, whatever the cost.

This is a fundamental element of being a disciple of Jesus Christ and essential if we are to enjoy the fullness of God's kingdom. God has made full provision for us through His Word and the power of the Holy Spirit. It is our decision to follow and obey Him that releases His power and blessing in our lives.

I have learned that love is a powerful motivator.

It brings tears to my eyes when I think of what I'm about to tell you.

During my first two years at Gordon's, I resented being there. I was angry with my parents, and I was particularly unkind to my mom. I didn't respond to her letters, and I never called her. During the holidays, I never kissed her and hardly spoke to her.

Nevertheless, my mom loved me through it all.

One day, my dad took me aside and explained to me how I was breaking my mom's heart. He told me that she would lay awake at night crying, worrying, and praying about me and whether they had made the right decision to send me away to Gordon's.

Hearing how I had hurt my mom touched my heart, and although it didn't happen overnight, I finally forgave her for sending me away to boarding school. Like the metamorphosis of a caterpillar into a butterfly, my motivation changed. I had a strong desire to make it up to my parents. I decided to work hard and play hard, to honor and please my parents. If they were happy with me, I would be happy.

In my fifth and final year at the school, my parents told me how proud they were of my achievements. Starting from a place of no position or responsibility, I was chosen to be head boy and sergeant major. Can you believe it? From being a rebel, I had the most senior position in the school.

In the headmaster's speech at the year-end ceremony, I was humbled to hear him say how well I had led the school. He told the parents and the boys that the school had a successful year in terms of morale, academics, sports, and discipline. It would be a year that no one would forget.

For me personally, it was a phenomenal year. I was the school champion in track and field (breaking the 400 meter, 800 meter, and javelin records), tennis, and chess. I represented the school in all the major sports and captained the soccer, field hockey, tennis, and track and field teams.

In 1985, I was invited back to Gordon's for its centenary. I went with Jeannie and baby Rebecca, and I led a number of former pupils as we marched past Queen Elizabeth and Prince Philip. My heart rose with pride. It was truly a day I will never forget.

If you are a parent, may I encourage you to never stop praying for your children. Keep thanking God for them and hold on to the hope you have for them in your heart. I'm so grateful that my parents never gave up and never stopped praying for me. My experience at Gordon's taught me priceless lessons that later helped me on my journey through the valley of suffering.

> *I have learned that living to love and please my parents, and my mom in particular, is powerful and rewarding.*
>
> *Later in life, I have learned that:*
>
> *- God wants my love for Him to be my motivation to live to please Him;*
>
> *- when I only live to please God, tremendous power is released for His will to be done and to live an abundant and content life.*

13.

Gifts and Abilities

One of the reasons I love to see great talent is that it gives a small glimpse of God's glory.

Listening to Beethoven or Bocelli, watching Usain Bolt break the 100-meter world record, or Lionel Messi dribble a football (soccer ball), seeing a sculpture by Michelangelo, or learning about the genius of Einstein or the lovingkindness of Mother Teresa, all give me joy, as I marvel at the gifts and abilities entrusted to them by Almighty God.

Everyone has been given a measure of gifts and abilities. We can't all be world champions or a great moral leader, but we can all influence and help at least one other person—especially when our talent extends to acts of kindness and goodness.

Sometimes, all it takes to encourage a person is a smile or a kind word. Anybody can do that. Some people have a heart of compassion, and they are able to serve the poor and the destitute.

> *I have learned that:*
>
> *- contentment and fulfillment is in applying my gifts and abilities to please God and do His will; and*
>
> *- when I only use my gifts and abilities for selfish reasons, at best I'm frustrated and discontent, and at worst, I hurt other people.*

From a young age, if I set my mind to do something, I didn't stop until I had achieved my goal. I know that the ability to focus and persevere are gifts that God has given to me. These, together with a competitive spirit, helped me to be successful in sports, academics, and work. The trouble is, in my youth, I applied these gifts purely for selfish reasons. Later in life, my singleness of heart for the Lord and my perseverance helped me to survive many storms.

Through my childhood, I felt so loved and secure, and being the youngest, my siblings encouraged me to try new and daring things. This gave me courage—the ability to have a go at new and challenging things. Courage is a wonderful gift when it is used for good. Unfortunately, in my early years, my courage, combined with my pride, got me into a lot of trouble.

Pride is one of the characteristics that most gets in the way of following Christ. In my teens and early 20s, I was full of pride, and looking back, I can see it robbed me of enjoying a full life. I'm defining pride as an unhealthy self-interest and belief that one is self-sufficient and independent. The Bible teaches the value of humility, which is the opposite of pride. Humility is the recognition of one's total dependence on God. It means being Christ-centered, whereas pride is self-centered.

I've discovered that a big part of Christ's work in my life is about denying self, understanding that it's all about Him, and learning to depend on Him. The Apostle Paul wrote,

I have been crucified with Christ; it is no longer I who live, but Christ lives in me; and the life which I now live in the flesh I live by faith in the Son of God, who loved me and gave Himself for me.

Galatians 2:20 NKJV

What do you think about being dependent on Christ? What does that look like for you today? In a culture that celebrates the selfmade person, it's quite a challenge to live in a way that recognizes your dependence on Christ.

Some people have told me I was a born leader. Leadership is a fantastic gift if people are being led in the right direction, but bad if not! I have a sensitivity to other people's emotions, and I have a gift to be able to discern how people are feeling. Today, this is often called "emotional intelligence," and it is the main reason that leaders progress in any organization.

Connected with emotional intelligence is a positive attitude. I'm more of a glass-half-full guy than half empty. I'm thankful for this. My heart's desire is to bless God and others, to encourage them and build them up. Generally, this is good, but Jeannie found this a great challenge when we were going through our deepest grief. One downside is that it can hinder you from being real and vulnerable with people and even with the Lord. I've discovered a better balance of being honest with my struggles and pain while also giving encouragement, by bringing things back to the Lord. David does this throughout the psalms.

I'm a visionary, and I know how to implement a vision. I have used the gift of planning and organizing throughout my life. I also know it can become a weakness when it comes to walking with the Lord. In the enthusiasm of my youth, I would think I could clearly see the way forward, and with my can-do attitude, I used to race ahead of the Lord!

> Over the years, I've learned to be still, to be in the moment, to enjoy every part of life, and to patiently wait for God's timing. I'm so grateful for God's patience with me!

I love the image of stillness in the following Scripture:

Blessed is the man who trusts in the LORD, and whose hope is the LORD. For he shall be like a tree planted by the waters, which spreads out its roots by the river, and will not fear when heat comes; But its leaf will be green, and will not be anxious in the year of drought, nor will cease from yielding fruit.

Jeremiah 17:7-8 NKJV

What gifts and abilities do you have? I believe your upbringing and your gifts and abilities give you a clue to God's purpose for your life. Make a list of the gifts and abilities that people have recognized in you. What have your parents, teachers, friends, work colleagues, and others said about you? Think outside the box. Maybe they commented on how your smile and your words encourage them. Maybe you have the gift of hospitality, or you have a wealth of knowledge and experience to share with others. What has God placed in your hands that you can use to help others?

Season Four—Passion with Purpose

Over 40 years, I have learned that if you follow Jesus, your desires and passions will lead you to God's purpose for your life.

Love and passion go together. I come alive when I'm living with passion, living from the love in my heart and not just the routine of life. Sometimes, our traditional piety leads us along a path that prevents us from experiencing the fullness of life that God intended.

I believe with all my heart that we are made for love—to receive and give love.

The ancient Greeks had three words for human love: *eros* (sexual love), *storge* (family love), and the highest form, *philia* (deep friendship and affection). God's love, *agape* love, is much more powerful and extends far beyond human love.

My ultimate passion, in the secret place of my soul, is to know Christ and to please Him by doing the things He has planned for me.

I've learned that following Christ is not about obeying rules and regulations but about living from the heart to please Him, because I love Him.

I still have a long way to go to please Christ, but my motivation is constant. It's God's love that is poured into my heart by the Holy Spirit (Romans 5:5).

God wants me to experience more and more of His love. Scripture says we need:

> *To grasp how wide and long and high and deep is the love of Christ and to know this love that surpasses knowledge.*
>
> ### Ephesians 3:18-19

God's love gives me freedom to be honest, to be real with myself and others. There is no control or manipulation in His love.

God's love changes my motivation. Instead of living for selfish desires, I only live to please God. Doing His will is my delight.

Jesus modeled this love and showed us how we should live. Jesus said,

> *I have come down from heaven not to do my will but the will of Him who sent me.*
>
> ### John 6:38

It gave Jesus great joy to please His father. Jesus is my role model. I want to live like He did.

God's will is that I love others. And it is more blessed to give than to receive. As a husband and father, I loved watching my wife and my children opening their presents on Christmas morning or on birthdays. Their joy in receiving gave me such joy in giving. I imagine that is how God feels about us.

I find there is something very inspiring and attractive in seeing someone living with passion for someone or something other than themselves. When that "someone" is Christ, you know that person will be in the sweet spot of God's purpose for their life.

14.

Who Are You Living For?

By my mid teens, my problem wasn't believing in Jesus; it was in living for Him. It was as though I had asked Him into my house (my life) but had left Him in the hallway. Every other room was for me and what I wanted—my career, pleasures, money, relationships, and so forth.

Another analogy is that I had invited Jesus to join me in my car, but I kept my hands on the steering wheel. I believed I had received the Holy Spirit, because no one can say Jesus is Lord without the Holy Spirit, but I was certainly not filled with the Holy Spirit. I was powerless and became more and more frustrated as a Christian.

The first disciples believed and put their trust in Jesus, but they didn't start living for Him until Pentecost, when they were filled with the Holy Spirit. From that point on, they had the power to live and eventually die for Him.

I'm wired to give 110 percent to whatever I am doing. I hate façades and I hate hypocrisy. As I was getting older, the lack of power in my Christian walk became a major problem. I was uncomfortable about being a Christian, and rather than tell my friends about Jesus, I hoped they wouldn't find out what I believed. Sunday was awkward because I was afraid one of my friends would see me going to church, or someone I knew might even see me in church. If friends came to tea, I would dread the moment when my mom would say grace before we ate. What on earth would my friends think of me!?

In my early teens, I would go to Christian camp, and my faith would be stirred. I would return home with grand intentions, but these would soon dissipate in the distractions, pressures, and pleasures of life.

> *I have learned that it's easy to say you believe in Christ, but it's another thing to live for Him.*

15.

Living for a False God

I had too much of the world in me to be at peace with the Lord, and I had too much of the Lord in me to be at peace in the world.

I knew what I had learned about Jesus was true, but I didn't have the strength to live for Him. Spiritually, I was in a bad place. I was frustrated by my hypocrisy.

I left the Gordon Boys' School when I was sixteen and studied for my A levels (university entrance exams) at a local high school. At this time, I decided to focus on my running. There is nothing wrong with that, but for me, it became like a god—I ate it, slept it, and drank it. My life revolved around running, and over time, it captured my heart. What gets your attention gets you! My running took the place of Christ, and I stopped going to church. I was living for a false god.

In high school; we sometimes discussed Christianity. I would speak up to say that Jesus was real and what was taught about Him was true. My friends would turn to look at me in shock and amazement. I realized my life was out of alignment with what I was saying. I was being a hypocrite.

I decided to stop trying to live for God. From that point on, it was all about me and what I wanted. I took full control of the steering wheel of my life, and I pushed God into the back seat.

I still believed in God, and I'm glad to say that I didn't blaspheme Him. But I was living a selfish life. I was just like the prodigal son. If anyone asked me, I would say I believed in God and Jesus, but as I would later realize, my selfish living was evidence of my unbelief. I believed enough to know God existed but not enough to live for Him.

Up to my early 20s, I knew Jesus as my Savior but not as my Lord.

Now that I was focused on my running, my 800-meter times started to improve rapidly. I was ranked second in my age group in the county (equivalent to a state in the U.S.) and was selected to go to the national championships.

Come rain, sleet, or snow, and no matter how tired I was after school, I would be out training. The cost was great. My muscles ached, my lungs burned, and I cut myself off from all distractions and all comforts. Nothing was going to get in between me and my running and achieving my goal. To me, the sacrifice was worth it.

On Sundays, I would have loved nothing better than to sleep in. But the training got even harder. The alarm would go off at 5:30 a.m., and I would travel two and a half hours to the National Track and Sports Center, Crystal Palace. It was a day of blood, sweat, and tears.

I felt so proud to be invited to join an elite national training squad, with one of the best coaches in the country. Most of the squad were my age, and some of them had won national championships and represented Great Britain at the junior level. It was a perfect situation to help me achieve my goal of reaching the top in athletics.

Sunday training was particularly tough. For the warm-up, we ran up a steep quarter-mile hill next to the stadium three times. We stretched and did drills before going to the track for the main session. This was intense, and if the guys didn't drop out, they would often be sick at the end of the repetitions. We had a short break for lunch, and then we lifted weights followed by a final session of relays and sprints on the grass. Then I traveled two and a half hours home, absolutely exhausted.

During this time, a friend pointed out a sponsored banking and finance course at Loughborough University, the top sports college in the country. They had an outstanding track team. The banking didn't appeal to me, but the opportunity to go to Loughborough was too good to be true. Enrollment in the course was full, but thankfully, I was accepted.

The Loughborough track team included national and international running stars, including Sebastian Coe, one of the greatest middle-distance runners of all time. I was in the ideal place to achieve my goal.

In my freshman year at Loughborough, I was picked for the varsity team. My running was going well. I came in third in the senior men's 800 meters at the South of England championships, was picked to run for the Southern Counties team, and was selected to run as a "hare" (to lead the race and set the pace) for two major televised track races. Included in the races were a few Olympic stars, such as John Walker and Steve Ovett, the top miler in the world, who won a gold medal at the 1980 Summer Olympics in Moscow.

In the Emsley Carr mile (an annual race that attracted top athletes from around the world), the sponsors wanted to see an under four minute mile, and my job was to take the worldclass field through the half-mile point in one minute 58 seconds. This was the first time I had run in front of 20,000 or so paying spectators and millions more on TV.

The gun went off, and I raced to the front to take up my role of setting the pace. Light bulbs flashed, and the crowd roared, and in that moment, I felt so proud to be leading the race. In fact, I could hardly believe it. I was feeling good. The only problem was, the other runners had decided to run slower than the agreed-upon pace. I glanced back; I had about 10 meters on the field, and I was opening up a gap.

The organizers and TV commentators were surprised to see me so far ahead after 600 meters, and they wondered if a shock result was on. The commentator started to announce my name to the crowd and encourage me to press on for the tape. Down the back straight for the penultimate time, I could hear Harry Wilson (Steve Ovett's coach) urging me on to the finish. At the bell, the start of the final lap, I was still leading, but I could hear the pack closing in on me. I would have loved to say I won the race, but it was not to be.

Ovett, the top miler in the world, won the race in under four minutes and congratulated me on a brave and lonely run. After the race, I was glad to be asked to be the hare in another televised race later that summer.

On the outside, my plans were going well. I was having success with my running, I had lots of great friends, a constant flow of girlfriends, and lots of fun, but I started to notice a nagging in my soul. Deep inside, my success was not fulfilling me.

16.

Love at First Sight

Although I was ignoring and hurting God, He still loved me, and He was after me. He had a plan to woo me back to Himself, and it would come about in a special way.

I was 20 years old when I first met Jeannie. It was a hot summer day, and I had arranged to go for a run with a friend. As I ran into his garden, there she was, smelling a rose. Although it was so many years ago, I will never forget when our eyes first met.

Jeannie was beautiful, with long dark hair and blue eyes. She was a professional ballerina—I noticed how slender she was. She had been trained at the Royal Ballet School, and was about to join a ballet company. The last thing she wanted was to fall in love. But somehow, Cupid's arrow reached her heart, and it was love at first sight.

I later realized that the matchmaker wasn't Cupid. Our attraction to each other was part of God's plan to woo me back to Himself. Jeannie and I were setting off on an unbelievable journey!

But I had two conflicts. First, my heart had become hardened in my fanatical pursuit of athletic achievement. I had pushed God and everyone else out, and there was no room in my heart for anyone or anything else.

Second, my friend had told me about Jeannie, and I assumed they were going out together. The strange thing was that he told me he thought we would get on well. Like two magnets connecting, a powerful force seemed to be drawing Jeannie and me together, but I needed to know about her relationship with my friend.

17.

Love at First Lunch

As part of my banking and finance degree course, I had to do six weeks of summer work in a Midland Bank branch. The day after our first meeting, I was serving on the front desk as a teller when to my surprise, I looked up, and there was Jeannie coming into the bank. She had her hair pulled back in a ponytail, and she looked even more beautiful than when we first met. I hadn't been able to get Jeannie out of my mind. I was excited to see her again.

I watched her walk to the back of the bank and then served my next customer. Jeannie joined the line for my teller position, and I felt excited as we were about to meet again. I looked up, and there she was, standing in front of me.

I thought she was going to do her banking, but she said, "We have things to discuss. Can we meet for a coffee?"

I was more than happy to meet Jeannie and answered, "Yeah, that would be great." It was nearly my lunch break, and we agreed to meet for a picnic lunch at the bowling green, down the road from the bank.

We met for our first lunch together, and we talked and laughed and had so much fun, as if we had known each other our whole lives. Jeannie made it clear that my friend was not her boyfriend. I was so pleased to hear this, and a weight seemed to fall off my shoulders. I was relaxed with Jeannie, and it seemed so natural to be together. From the beginning, it was as though we were soul mates.

I later talked with my friend about Jeannie.

"I always thought you two would get on," he said. Finally, I felt I was free to become romantically involved with Jeannie.

I remember our first kiss. We had arranged to meet along the seafront by the fishpond in Westleigh Gardens. There was a full moon, its silvery light shimmered across the ocean to where we were. The stars sparkled in the night sky. It felt so good to finally take Jeannie in my arms. We had our first kiss.

The year was 1978. We had a summer romance. We were inseparable and worked our days around our summer jobs and our training. Everything was so exciting! We watched sunrises and sunsets, went for walks along the beach and in the countryside, and ended up in cozy pubs for candlelit dinners. Just a girl and a boy in a bubble of love.

But sadly, time ticked on, the summer drew to an end, and Jeannie and I had to go our separate ways—she to a ballet company overseas and me to my second year at Loughborough University.

We had our last kiss and promised to write every day while we were apart.

18.

Back to College

Memories of my time with Jeannie over the summer were special to me. I missed Jeannie so much, and I loved it when I received one of her letters. My days were busy and went by quickly.

In my second year at Loughborough University, I was made vice-captain of the track and field team. All my hard training started to pay off. My 800-meter times continued to improve. I won the England and Wales universities' 800-meter title and recorded what would turn out to be my best times, 1 minute 50.4 seconds for 800-meter and 3 minutes 48 seconds for 1,500-meter races.

After only four years of proper training, I was one of the fastest 800-meter runners in the country for my age, and I was on course to reach my goal to run in the Olympics.

My entrepreneurial spirit also kicked in, and I made quite a bit of money selling sweatshirts and T-shirts on campus. The plan was to expand the business to other university campuses and eventually launch a health and fitness business.

Suddenly, my second year at Loughborough was over. I was home, and I couldn't wait to see Jeannie again. We had another romantic summer together.

19.

A Big Year and a Big Change

I returned to Loughborough for my final year, and Jeannie went back overseas to dance.

It was 1979 and I was now captain of the university track and field team. It was the strongest student team in the country, including international athletes like megastar Sebastian Coe. Earlier that year, Seb broke the 800-meter, 1,500-meter, and one-mile world records, in the space of 41 days. The following year was the Summer Olympics in Moscow, where he won gold in the 1,500-meter and silver in the 800-meter races. And he was running on my team!

Because of the distractions on campus, I decided to share an off-campus house so I could focus on my running and my finals. I threw myself headlong into my training. It was going well; I managed to train twice a day for a few days a week. I was in great shape, but then one Sunday, during my second training session of the day, I strained my Achilles tendon, one of the worst injuries for an athlete. I hated getting injured. Athletics was my god, and when I couldn't run, I got frustrated.

My running had such a hold on my life; I wondered how I would ever be free of it!

Although I didn't appreciate it at the time, God had me exactly where He wanted me. He had a few things He wanted to say to me, and it seemed as though He was gently putting His finger under my chin to lift up my head so He could have my attention.

I couldn't run because of my injury, I was away from the distractions of campus life, and Jeannie was away dancing. I was on my own and in a place where I could hear from God.

I hated my circumstances, but they proved to be a turning point in my life. I started to read my Bible again. I began to question my values and my selfish lifestyle. As I read the Bible, the following verse jumped out at me:

The thief has come to rob, kill and destroy but I have come to give you life and life in abundance.

John 10:10

That Scripture seemed to stir something deep in my heart. At the end of the summer, Jeannie had raised the question of marriage. We were so in love, and to her, the obvious next step was to get married. But the plans I had for my life didn't include marriage.

My plans were based on the values of the world and they didn't include being tied into a relationship. If I continued along the path I was on, my relationship with Jeannie was probably going to end.

Something seemed terribly wrong with the way of the world. I remembered Jesus' words: "What does it benefit a man if He gains the whole world and yet forfeits his soul?" (Mark 8:36). This made sense to me. You can have everything on the outside—money, fame, power—but if you're miserable and have no peace on the inside, what have you gained?

I was going to be giving up the relationship I had with Jeannie to gain things on the outside, but they might not fulfill me on the inside. My logic seemed to be flawed.

Things came to a head on February 14, 1980. Yes, it was Valentine's Day, which I think reflects God's heart to woo me into a relationship with Him. The day before, I received a letter from my brother Will. Like me, he had turned his back on God. He chose the hippie and drug lifestyle. All of my siblings turned from God for a time and tested our parents severely. While traveling the world in a search for the meaning of life, Will was moved by the beauty of creation, and he recommitted his life to Jesus Christ.

"I know you have a plan for your life," Will wrote in his letter, "but I want you to know that God has a plan for your life made out of perfect love."

I had never received a letter from Will before. The logic of his words made sense to me. The timing of his letter made them all the more meaningful. I had come to a fork in the road. Should I continue with my plan or change to God's path for my life? I thought my plan was good, but how on earth could I compete with the Creator of the universe?

I realized I was seeing only a fraction of what was going on today and what might happen tomorrow, but God sees everything. I could see that my plan might look good now, but around the corner I might run into a roadblock or a different set of circumstances. I pictured it like a mouse in a maze. The mouse thinks it's doing well, but just around the corner is a dead end. The mouse can't see it, but you can see it because you are looking from above the maze. In the same way, God knows exactly what is ahead. In fact, He is over all things and has planned all things to fulfill His eternal plan and purpose.

The next morning, I was sitting at my desk thinking about Will's letter. The atmosphere seemed to change. God spoke to me. His voice wasn't audible, but it was so clear in my heart that I knew it was God.

These are the words that God spoke to my heart. "Gerard, I love you, and I have a plan for your life made out of perfect love. If you let Me, I will show you this plan. You may not get the things you want on the outside, but I promise, I will give you quality of life on the inside."

It was like a light was turned on in my soul.

I had a clear choice. God had brought me to this point, and He was calling me to follow and serve Him.

God was so real to me in that moment, and the path to take seemed so obvious. I would have been out of my mind to say no to God at that point! I did what the Bible calls repentance. Inside, I made a conscious decision to turn around from the way I was going, and I surrendered myself wholeheartedly to follow Jesus Christ and to do His will.

There was no music playing, no Christians present, just a young man making a clear decision to make Jesus the Lord of his life. At that moment, the atmosphere in the room felt sacred. I was aware of God's presence and He touched my heart.

I hadn't cried for seven or eight years—my heart had been hardened by pride and selfishness—but I began to sob like a baby. It felt as though God was wrapping His arms around me and soaking me in His love. It was like liquid love, and it was filling my heart and my whole being.

About half an hour later, the most incredible joy welled up from within me as though I had arrived at my purpose for living. I had found the reason for being on earth. It was to serve and glorify God. I had complete trust in God's hand on and over my life. It was as if I had jumped off a cliff and into His arms. Whatever life held for me, I would be okay, because He was with me.

It was a powerful experience, and it instantly transformed me in several ways.

First and most important, I fell head over heels in love with Jesus Christ. My one burning motivation was to please Him, and that has remained to this day. It completely changed the course of my life.

Second, the Bible came alive to me, mainly because in it I could learn more about the lover of my soul, Jesus Christ. I couldn't put it down. I would read it late into the night, making copious notes.

Third, I had to tell other people about Jesus. This had nothing to do with any obligation but because I was overflowing with love for Him. The natural thing, when you have fallen in love with someone, is to tell other people about it.

Fourth, without even thinking about it, I stopped swearing. I seemed to have been washed from the inside out.

And fifth, my running had lost its hold on me. My heart was so filled with love for Jesus Christ that everything else was secondary.

I now understand that I had been filled with the Holy Spirit. This was similar to what happened to the disciples at Pentecost and to other disciples, as recorded in the Acts of the Apostles (Acts 2:1-13, 4:31, and 9:17).

> *I have since come to learn that being filled with the Holy Spirit should not be a one-off occurrence, but as the Apostle Paul wrote,*

"Don't get drunk on wine, but be filled with the Holy Spirit" (the original Greek means an ongoing filling). D.L. Moody, one of the greatest evangelists of the 19th century, summed it up well when he said, "I need to keep on being filled with the Holy Spirit because I leak."

The Holy Spirit had poured God's love into my heart (Romans 5:5). I only wanted to live for God and to do His will. I was desperate for other people to see and meet Jesus Christ as I had, to experience His love and the sense of completeness that He gives.

I had found a gold mine with enough gold for everyone, and I needed to tell everyone about it.

In my athletics, I had a clear goal, and I didn't allow anything to distract me. I applied the same approach to my Christian walk. The goal was clear—to love and know Jesus more and more, and to love and make Him known to others. I understood that Christ, by the Holy Spirit, was actually within me, and if I was going to know Him more and make Him known to others, I had to do what the Bible calls "decrease"—I had to die to self, to get out of the way (Galatians 2:20). Jesus said,

I tell you the truth, unless an ear of wheat falls to the ground and dies, it remains only a single seed. But if it dies, it produces many seeds. The man who loves his life will lose it, while the man who hates his life in this world will keep it for eternal life. Whoever serves me must follow me; and where I am, my servant also will be. My father will honor the one who serves me.
John 12:24-26

God has wired me a certain way, to be 100 percent on the path I'm on, and it seemed natural for me to pray:

"Lord, please break me down that I may know You more and that You would show Your glory through me."

I have prayed this prayer ever since that day. It is the prayer of my life!

My prayer is that everyone will experience God's presence and His love, just as I have.

> *I learned that there comes a time in life when one has to make a courageous decision to accept the call and break away from every hindrance and sin, and to step into the unknown with God.*

Do you have peace that you are following the right plan and purpose for your life? Do you believe God is the source of life and that He loves you? What, if anything, is holding you back from surrendering your life to God?

20.

Finding My Purpose

In William Shakespeare's As You Like It, one of the characters says this: "All the world's a stage, and all the men and women merely players; they have their exits and their entrances; and one man in his time plays many parts, his acts being seven ages."

Through my encounter with God, it was as though I was entering the most important story—God's story for humankind. God had written a part in His story just for me! It was a part that He had been preparing me for, something unique and special. I felt fully alive and overflowing with anticipation. I was starting out on a great adventure, a great mission.

In his book Wild at Heart, John Eldredge does a masterful job of explaining the secret of a man's soul: "Deep in his heart, every man longs for a battle to fight, an adventure to live, and a beauty to rescue. That is how he bears the image of God: that is what God made him to be."

God had called me to live for a mission that is greater than myself. To live with passion. To be a warrior who is willing to lay his life down for his king.

I wanted to follow as closely as I could in the steps of my champion, Jesus Christ, who lived a life surrendered to the will of His Father.

In studying the Bible, I was in awe of Jesus' character. He showed me how to love. He revealed to me how to be faithful in the face of great opposition and how to care for the poor and the downtrodden. He modeled what real courage is, when, knowing He was about to be tortured and put to death on the cross, He said to His Father, "Not My will but Yours be done." He sacrificed His life for me, so I could live and be with Him for eternity!

Jesus' love and character stir my heart from deep within and inspire me to want to follow Him. I have the same desire as the Apostle Paul who said:

I want to know Christ—yes, to know the power of his resurrection and participation in his sufferings, becoming like him in his death.

Philippians 3:10

This is risky living. It's dangerous. It could cost me my life. But this, I believe, is the ultimate purpose for my life. God wants me to live on earth as an alien and a stranger, to be His hands and feet, to help rescue the souls of men, women, and children.

My mission had been given to me. I wanted to share Jesus' love with as many people as I could.

21.

Sharing My Faith

In my first seventeen years as a Christian, I was terrified to tell anyone about my faith in Christ. With the transformation of my heart, I now had a passion and boldness to tell people about Jesus Christ. I decided to start with my friends and the first one was Graham.

"Graham, I want to tell you of something that has happened to me," I started, rather nervously, and went on to explain about Will's letter and how I had questioned my values. I told him, "I have decided to follow Jesus Christ and His plan for my life."

I could see the shock on Graham's face, which I could understand. He knew me as one of the lads, captain of the track team, and a good friend, and here I was telling him that I was living for Jesus Christ and His will for my life. As I continued talking to him, joy flowed from within. I smiled from ear to ear!

The joy grew as I told my story to hundreds of others over the next few weeks. No one ever mocked me to my face, although they may have done so behind my back! I was okay with that, though. I was so in love with Jesus Christ, I didn't mind what people thought of me, and the more I spoke about Him in public, the more the joy flowed.

A mission was being held on campus, featuring a speaker named Eric Delve.

I asked him if I could tell my testimony in one of the big meetings. He said yes, and so I invited everyone I could think of and was delighted when my friends and my family said they would come.

The sun was shining on the big day, and I was excited to tell my testimony, but I was also terrified. I had a problem, because I had not spoken in public since a school debate years before when I forgot everything I was going to say. Quite honestly, it was a disaster. My nerves were worse than before a race, and I shook as the adrenalin pumped through me. When I was called up to speak, I went to leap up on the stage. Normally, this would have been easy for me, but not this time. I caught my foot on the edge and fell flat on my face in front of everyone. My friends, in good humor, gave a great roar of laughter, but the fall actually served me well. It knocked all the nervousness out of me, and I was able to tell my story without forgetting anything.

God's love filled my heart. I would do anything to please Him, not out of duty but because it was my heart's delight to bring Him pleasure, to bring a smile to His face.

I wanted to live a holy life, a life separated to His will. Someone described this as similar to his love for his wife. He didn't want to do anything that would bring a shadow of disappointment across her face. The Apostle Paul described this as follows: "For Christ's love compels us, because we are convinced that one died for all and therefore all died. And he died for all, that those who live should no longer live for themselves but for him who died for them and was raised again" (2 Corinthians 5:14-15).

I believe that the only motivation strong enough to inspire a person to lay down their life for God is His love, which is "poured into our hearts by the Holy Spirit" (Romans 5:5).

In handing my life over to God, I had peace that He was in control. I was inspired and energized in the knowledge that He had a plan and purpose for my life. My mind was being renewed daily in God's Word, and His love drove all worry and fear from my heart. This set me free to trust God in this new start to my life.

Have you ever had an experience of the Holy Spirit pouring God's love into your heart? If so, what difference did it make in your life?

22.

Jeannie

I was eager to tell Jeannie what happened to me. We were already in the habit of writing love letters to each other—this was before cell phones and computers—so I wrote a long letter to Jeannie telling her about my encounter with God and how I had been transformed. I told her I had given my heart to Christ, and my new goal in life was to love and follow Him.

A few days later, I received an early morning call from Jeannie. She had received my letter and was concerned. She had to talk to me.

I loved hearing her voice, but I could tell she was anxious to hear some more about what happened. I explained the encounter I had with God and how it felt like liquid love had been poured into my heart. There was a silence, and then Jeannie asked in all sincerity, "Does this mean you're going to become a monk?"

"No, Jeannie," I replied, laughing. "But I have had a dramatic change in my life, and I am now living for Jesus Christ."

There was another silence, and then Jeannie asked, "How does this affect us?"

"Jeannie," I said. "I believe God does want us to be together."

I heard a sob. "That's such a relief," Jeannie said.

We said our goodbyes and made plans to see each other later in the spring. I'll just say, springtime in England is beautiful with flowers, fragrances, songbirds and new life.

Over the years, people have asked me, "How do you know who is the right one to marry?"

This is how I knew.

I prayed, "Lord, You know I love Jeannie, but I only want to live for Your will in my life. Lord, if Jeannie is the one for me to marry, please give me a burden to pray for her, but if she is not the right one for me, I surrender her to You."

After praying, I had such a burden for Jeannie, I would often cry as I prayed for her. During the time she was away, I had three impressions that I believed were from the Lord.

First, I saw Jeannie climbing a giant beanstalk (similar to the fairy-tale "Jack and the Beanstalk"), looking over her shoulder, and laughing and smiling. Jeannie later told me that in the early days away, although she missed me, life was new and exciting.

The second thing I saw was Jeannie sitting on top of the beanstalk, laughing and looking very happy. At this time, Jeannie reached what she had been working so hard to achieve. She was succeeding professionally, appearing on TV, and leading a glamorous life. She had reached her goals.

In the third and final phase, I saw that Jeannie had fallen off the beanstalk and was looking sad and disappointed. At this time, Jeannie realized that after achieving her professional dancing goals, she was asking herself, "Is this it, then?" She felt unfulfilled.

Like Jeannie, have you ever had a time in your life when you were climbing your own "beanstalk"? Perhaps you thought you would find fulfillment in a person, a job, or a place but were later disappointed.

Finally, spring came, and Jeannie and I were together again. We would have Easter together before I went back to Loughborough University to sit for my finals.

Jeannie told me I looked different, as if a light was shining on me. The longer we were together, she could see I had great joy. But, she didn't understand why I loved the Bible and why I was always talking about Jesus.

I didn't know how best to tell Jeannie about Christ and I prayed, "Lord, please help me to share my faith with Jeannie." I knew she loved poetry, so I got creative and suggested we read the book of Proverbs together, going through the wise and inspiring words in each chapter. We would go for walks in the countryside and end up sitting round an open fire in an old pub, drinking tomato juice with a dash of Worcestershire sauce for Jeannie and a beer for me. I would take out my Bible and read Proverbs to Jeannie. One day, we were approached by a lady in one of our favorite pubs.

"How romantic," she said. "You're reading your girlfriend some poetry!" We thanked the lady. Little did she know what she had just said, and I smiled at Jeannie.

I was on fire for God, and every Sunday I would go to a church service that was similar to what we read about in the Acts of the Apostles. The Bible teaches that Christ followers are strengthened through the gifts of the Holy Spirit, such as teaching, preaching, words of knowledge, tongues, and prophecy. The atmosphere in the services was full of love and joy, the singing and harmony moved me to tears, and a two- to three-hour service seemed like only a few minutes.

Each Sunday, I would invite Jeannie to come to the service, but she refused me each time. On my last Sunday before returning to Loughborough, although it seemed like the eleventh hour, I thought I might as well ask Jeannie one more time.

"Jeannie," I said, "it's our last Sunday together for a while. Please, will you come to church with me?"

To my surprise, she said yes. I took Jeannie in my arms and whispered "thank you" in her ear. Jeannie later told me she had no intention of going to church and was surprised when she heard herself agreeing to go with me. My prayers had been answered. I was so excited to take Jeannie to my church. It was a beautiful spring morning when I went to pick up Jeannie for the Sunday service, and as you might imagine, I was a little apprehensive as to how Jeannie would react. I needn't have been concerned, though, because the Lord had already made provision for her. My brother's wife, Sue, sat next to Jeannie, and before the service started, she whispered to her, "Just have an open mind!"

I was tempted to keep checking to see how Jeannie was getting on, but I felt the Lord say to me, "You keep your eyes on Me, and I will take care of Jeannie." It was another powerful service that went on for more than two hours. I loved it, but I wondered what Jeannie would make of it.

At the end of the service, she said to me, "Gerard, now I know what you've been talking about!"

Jeannie came to faith in Christ that morning, and God gave her a new heart and put His Holy Spirit within her. I could now share my love and joy in Jesus with Jeannie. We were on the same page.

How open are you to hear from God in different ways, such as through a dream? Dreams are mentioned several times in the Bible. What experiences, if any, have you had of dreams that might have been from God? What do you think about denominations and non-denominational churches? How do you think God might be using different denominations?

23.

"Will You Marry Me?"

I was having dreams about marrying Jeannie and people often commented about how in love we were. Even my old coach, who lived as though he had no faith in God, said that Jeannie and I seemed to be spiritually united. Most of all, I couldn't imagine life without her by my side.

When she came to faith in Christ, I knew the way was open for us to marry, but I couldn't see us getting engaged until after I graduated and settled into my first job. But God had other plans.

I was learning to hear God's voice, and He would often give me a verse for whatever situation I was in. Each verse would be exactly right for me, and I started to grow in my faith. Prayer was an important part of my day. One day, as I knelt beside my bed, I felt God tell me that I should propose to Jeannie. It didn't make a lot of sense to propose at that time. I was only 22 years old, I still had my finals to complete, and I had a lot of responsibility as captain of the track and field team.

I said to the Lord, "Lord, You know how much I love Jeannie, and I believe You have planned for us to be one in marriage, but I need to know this is the right time to propose to her. Please give me a clear Scripture."

Straightaway I sensed the Lord say to me, "Read Joshua chapter 10 and chapter 8."

I eagerly read Joshua 10. In verse 5 were the words "joined forces," which I took to confirm that Jeannie and I should marry. I then read chapter eight. Verse eight said, "Do what the Lord has commanded. See to it; you have my orders!"

I suspect you may be skeptical. After all, would God speak to someone in this way? I can understand you thinking this. I agree that we have to be careful in picking out Scriptures to confirm what we already want to do and then saying, "God led me this way."

But I hadn't picked out the Scriptures, and the great passion of my heart was to do God's will, even if this meant giving up Jeannie.

Immediately after reading the Bible passages, I rang Jeannie and asked if she could meet me at one of our favorite spots on the seafront. She later told me that earlier that day, it occurred to her that I was going to propose to her, but it still came as a surprise.

We walked hand in hand, and at a quiet spot, I held Jeannie in my arms, and looking into her beautiful blue eyes, I said, "Jeannie, I love you. I want to live the rest of my life with you. Please, will you marry me?"

One of the reasons I love Jeannie is her free spirit. She often surprises people by what she says and does. In our romantic moment, Jeannie replied to my proposal by saying, "Pardon, what did you say?"

Laughing, I said to Jeannie again, "Jeannie, I love you, and I want to live the rest of my life with you. Please, will you marry me?"

With tears in her eyes and a big smile, Jeannie answered, "Yes."

We didn't have long to celebrate, because later that day we headed to Crystal Palace for a big 1,500-meter race. I had a special spring in my running that night, and I won the race.

After a final farewell to Jeannie and to my parents, I headed off to Loughborough for my finals and a big track season.

What experiences have you had in receiving a Scripture that helped guide you on your journey? List three Scriptures that have helped direct you in your life.

24.

Mistakes

I have done things in my past that I regret. Perhaps you have too.

Bad decisions can have consequences that stay with us for years. But, the good news is that God is able to turn our worst mistakes into something good. Instead of leaving us with a weakness that debilitates us, God is able to use our mistakes as part of our destiny to help others.

Don't let the mistakes in your life hold you back from coming into the destiny that God has planned for you. Surrender every part of your life, including your mistakes, to God, and He will take your life and use it powerfully for His eternal plan and purpose.

In learning to walk with God, I made many mistakes, none bigger than what I am about to tell you.

Someone once said that a young person freshly filled with the Holy Spirit needs to be closely discipled, because in their passion for God and their eagerness to please Him, they are vulnerable to Satan's deception.

The first signs of Satan deceiving me appeared shortly after I had the encounter with God. I had been asked to audition to be an extra in the film *Chariots of Fire*. However, because I felt my running had such a hold on me in the past, I didn't want to do anything that might distract me from my walk with Christ. I decided to decline the offer.

In hindsight, this was a bad decision that pointed to an overly religious spirit that wanted to confine my life, rather than enjoying Jesus' abundant life. *Chariots of Fire* is now one of Jeannie's and my favorite films. We have watched it several times over. It would have been fun to be in the movie.

Around this same time, Jeannie wanted to set a wedding date. I had not given our wedding date any thought. I prayed about the date and felt the Lord showed me three signs that had to happen before we got married. The first was that I would win the 800 meters in the AAA (Amateur Athletic Association) vs. Loughborough student race later that summer. Second, I would finish my exams, and third, I would be transferred within the bank. I had decided that after college, I would continue on the executive management course with Midland Bank.

I shared with Jeannie the three signs that I felt God had given me. She said it was all a bit of a mystery to her, because all she wanted was a date.

Everything inside me wanted to please the Lord and be obedient to what I felt He had told me, but it troubled me to see Jeannie struggling with my reluctance to set a wedding date, until the three signs had occurred.

I believe every new Christian should have a mentor and pastoral covering to help them discern what is from God and what is from Satan. I didn't have a mentor or a pastoral covering, and Satan outwitted me.

I was filled with such love and joy at this time, and God's Word was so alive to me, it didn't cross my mind that I had made a mistake over the three signs.

I have learned that things can be going well, and yet we can have blind spots in our lives where Satan is deceiving us.

Jeannie and my family and friends were not quite sure what to make of the three signs. Things were about to get worse.

In my love for God I wanted everyone to hear about Jesus Christ, and I started a radio show on the university campus. I played Christian music, taught the Bible, and interviewed people.

Thinking the three signs were from God, I announced on the university radio that I felt God had told me I was going to win the 800-meter race in the upcoming AAA vs. Loughborough athletics meeting. That might have sounded reasonable—except for the fact Sebastian Coe would be in the race!

I have learned that when we make a mistake, if we don't get back on the right path quickly, we end up exacerbating the situation by making more mistakes.

As I think back to this bizarre time, I cringe at what a fool I had been, but I also thank God that He didn't abandon me.

As the race drew nearer, more and more people heard about my prediction. Several Christians on and off campus contacted me and tried to persuade me to back off. Unfortunately, I was fully committed, believing God would empower me to win the race.

To prepare myself for what I believed God was going to do, I decided to fast for five days and not drink for two days before the race! Also, instead of running in my spikes, I would run in my training shoes, which had far less grip.

If you're thinking I was fanatical, you would be right. I was genuinely sincere in what I was doing, but I was sincerely wrong! Here's what happened.

The day of the race was hot, and Jeannie and I walked up into the hills. We held hands, but we walked in silence as I tried to stay focused. God was going to come through and show His power. I remember looking up into the blue sky with the wispy clouds and sensing God's nearness.

I warmed up for the race. Seb wished me all the best (I think he had heard about my prediction). This was the biggest athletics event on the university calendar, and it attracted a large crowd plus TV coverage. The atmosphere was building, and my heart was pounding.

It was time, and we headed down to the start. The starter asked us to strip off our tracksuits and to line up on the starting line. I heard a gasp from some of my friends in the crowd. They told me later it was because I looked so much thinner!

The gun went off, and I ran a fast 400 meters in my trainers and was not far off the pace. But, about 50 meters into the third 200 meters, my body started to shut down. It was a very strange feeling, as my muscles jerked and strained.

I collapsed at 600 meters. I was semiconscious, but I remember some of my friends racing across the infield and half carrying me back to the start.

I was humiliated, and rightly so. I had been an idiot and had caused great concern and worry for Jeannie and my friends. I apologized to Jeannie for my mistake and for causing her so much anxiety, but I wish I had done a better job of apologizing to other people! Jeannie was kind and understanding and said, "I'm just glad that you are alive!"

A Christian friend and student pastor drove Jeannie and me back to my house. I sat quietly in a chair, and I think the others were concerned that I might need to go to the hospital. I pondered what had just happened and wondered why the outcome was so different from what I thought I had heard from God. The answer came through a friend, a man in his early 30s, who was married with two children. He sat on the ground and encouraged me. He reassured me and said that in my heart, I had been obedient to what I thought God had shown me, and I was willing to risk my reputation for the glory of God.

I could have died in the race, but in God's mercy, I recovered quickly— so quickly that in the evening, I took my place as team captain at the university banquet and delivered a speech as though nothing had ever happened. As it would turn out, I sat next to Seb at the banquet. At the end of the day, I was grateful for the opportunity to tell him about my faith in Christ and why I had made the prediction about the race.

God loves us, even when we make bad mistakes. I told the Lord I was sorry for what I had done, and I knew He had forgiven me.

> *I have learned that even when I feel close to God and everything is going well, I need to be accountable and keep wise, godly counsel with trusted friends.*

What mistakes have you made that you regret? Have you told God and anyone else impacted by your action that you are sorry? Be gentle with yourself, because we all make mistakes. Know that God has forgiven you. Move on from your mistakes and know that God can turn them around for good.

25.

Bizarre Encounters

I completed my finals at Loughborough, and my parents and Jeannie joined me for graduation day and a special celebration dinner as I received my BSc (honors) degree in banking and finance.

It felt so good to be going home after a busy semester. I was so excited to have some more time with Jeannie before I started my banking career in London.

During this time, something bizarre happened to us.

Early one morning while the tide was out, Jeannie and I decided to go for a walk on the beach, close to where I had proposed to her. On our way there, we were holding hands, chatting, and laughing when a strange woman started screaming at Jeannie.

"Don't marry him! Don't marry him!!" she screamed.

"Do you know who she is?" I asked.

"No, I've never seen her before in my life," Jeannie whispered.

As the woman continued to rant and rave from across the road, Jeannie nestled into me, and without responding to the woman, I said,

"Just ignore her." With my arm around Jeannie, we continued on down to the beach.

It was a magnificent morning. We took off our shoes and ran over the sand to where the sea was slowly lapping up on the beach. As so often happens on our walks, we laughed and kissed and chased each other. We were so in love; it was beautiful.

Suddenly, from across the beach we heard another woman shouting and screaming at us.

"What are you doing? You shouldn't be together! Whatever you do, don't get married!"

This strange-looking woman—not the one who screamed at us earlier— was standing on the promenade and saying similar things.

Grabbing my arm, Jeannie said, "Gerard, this is odd. What's going on?" "I'm not sure," I said, "but both of the women sound as though they are demon-possessed."

As a young Christian, I had no experience with demon-possessed people, but I had read about them in the Bible and in Christian books, and I had had some teaching about them in church. It was so peculiar that on the same morning, two women we had never met before should start ranting and raving at us about not getting married.

What do you think about our experience with these two odd women? Perhaps you have experienced people or events that were rather weird. Do you believe there are demonic forces that operate on earth to "rob, kill and destroy" (John 10:10) and who try to keep us from knowing God?

26.

New Beginnings in London

It was a step of faith when Jeannie and I decided to be based in London and for me to continue the executive management program at the bank. In one sense, it was a sacrifice, because we had to leave our family and friends, the country life that we loved so much, and the sports and outdoor lifestyle. However, we both had peace that this was the right step for us. It was our calling. As we stepped out in faith, we were filled with joy, and we knew we were in the sweet spot of God's will.

It was September 1980 and I was excited as I started my first assignment as a foreign clerk in the Queen Victoria Street bank branch in the City (London's finance and insurance district).

I enjoyed my first job, and I worked hard, but I also prayed for an opportunity to tell my colleagues about my encounter with God and my faith in Christ.

I did have some good spiritual conversations, and although I didn't see any real fruit, I prayed that God would use my words to draw people to Himself. One conversation was with a big guy named

Stephen, who told me he didn't know if there was a God. But, after the birth of his daughter, he made a point of telling me that he went outside and looking up, said, "God, if You're up there, I want to say, 'Thank You.'"

> *I learned that birth, along with death and marriage, are spiritual events and often a time when God reaches out His hand of love to touch people's hearts.*

Finding accommodation in London can be a real challenge. After I prayed about it, a door opened for me to rent a flat in the Barbican, an affluent residential area close to my office. Starting on a relatively low salary, I would never have been able to afford such a luxurious flat, but a friend of a friend let me rent it for a reasonable price. It was the first and only time in my banking career that I could walk to work and pop home at lunchtime. On Wednesdays, I was allowed to study at home for the Institute of Banking exams.

For the first month in London, I visited various churches, looking for the one God wanted me to serve in. I decided to settle in a church that was similar to the one I had been attending in my home town. The congregation was made up of young people who, like me, were hungry to know Jesus more and to serve Him however they could.

Jeannie had been delayed in moving up to London for a few months and I was excited when she joined me. Continuing her ballet training, she shared a flat in West Hampstead with a girl from the church. Jeannie came over to see me every day, and it was always so difficult when she had to leave in the evening.

Since my encounter with God, Jeannie and I stopped sleeping together. I lived to please God, and I knew He had designed sex to be beautiful but also sacred within marriage. After Jeannie came to faith in Christ, we both wanted to honor God in our relationship.

You'll be pleased to hear that we set a date for our wedding in the spring.

27.

Wedding Day

I woke up on April 4, 1981, and noticed the birds were singing outside my window, as though they knew it was my wedding day. I felt so alive. This was our big day!

We were married in a small Baptist church up the road from Jeannie's home. The cherry blossoms and spring flowers were blooming outside the church, speaking of new life in every leaf.

My bride looked radiant. She stood beside me at the front of the church, and I looked over to her beautiful face behind her lace veil. Typical Jeannie—she blew me a kiss.

We felt the presence of the Lord as we made our vows before God. As Mr. and Mrs. Long, we were together as one, on the journey God had prepared for us.

Walking out of the church, we loved seeing the smiling faces of our friends and family as they threw confetti.

The last lines of the hymn "When I Survey the Wondrous Cross"—"Love so amazing so divine"—describe what I felt on my wedding day. Jeannie and I took to heart the last line of the hymn as we embraced God's calling on our lives —"Demands my soul, my life, my all."

We had a cozy, intimate reception in Jeannie's home.

My college friends had fun decorating our car with the traditional tin cans and balloons and words to make sure everyone knew we were "Just Married." Our friends and family waved and cheered as we drove off into the sunset. Driving through the countryside, we came to a quaint old hotel in the New Forest called The Angel. The day ended with a romantic candlelit dinner. Knowing how much it would mean to Jeannie, I reserved a table overlooking a fountain (we had our first kiss by a fountain).

Holding hands, we went upstairs to the bridal suite. It was so romantic, so unreal, one of the best days of my life.

Season Five—How to Walk by Faith

In Season Four, I told you how God had worked to bring me back to Himself, how He had given me a clear purpose to share His love with others, and how Jeannie and I had married and were starting out on an exciting journey with Him. Jeannie and I were totally committed to give "our lives, our all" to love and follow Jesus.

In reality, it meant we had to learn to walk by faith.

Scripture teaches that the only way to please God is to walk by faith (Hebrews 11:6). That meant we had to learn to trust God in practical ways in everyday life—for example, with our finances, our home, our careers, and our family.

It's easy to trust God when everything is going well, but the real test of our faith and our love for God comes when things don't go according to plan.

Thankfully, as a loving heavenly Father, God was going to develop and grow our faith as we walked with Him.

One of the wonders of the early years of a child's life is the total dependence and trust in the parents. The love of the parents provides a beautiful environment for children to develop and blossom in their God-given gifts and abilities.

Learning to take those first few steps is a bit like learning to walk by faith—with mom and dad nearby, encouraging the young child to keep going, saying, "You can do it." Yes, the child has a few falls, but he or she quickly gets up and tries again. Gradually, the muscles and the trust develop enough, and the child begins to walk one step at a time.

To grow in our relationship with God and to come into His purpose for us, we learned through our everyday life that we could trust Him. We learned that what He has said in His Word, the Bible, is true and can be relied on.

Now faith is confidence in what we hope for and assurance about what we do not see.

Hebrews 11:1

When things don't work out as we expect, we learn that God is doing something bigger than we can see or understand. God's ways are so much higher than our ways (Isaiah 55:8-9), and He is always working for His glory and our good.

It's because God loves us so much that He tests and refines our faith, preparing us for the work He has assigned to us, in this age and through eternity.

In this season, I am going to tell you how God caused my faith to go deep, like roots, into His abundant life, giving me a strong foundation for future storms.

28.

Our First Homes

I carried Jeannie over the threshold of our first home in the Barbican. Jeannie gasped and said, "You've brought me to a flower shop!" I had filled our apartment with flowers, and the fragrance was intoxicating. We were so happy. I took my bride into my arms and kissed her.

A few weeks later, we were overjoyed when we discovered that Jeannie was pregnant. But we had not figured that we would have to move so soon, because our landlord decided to move back into the apartment we occupied.

We prayed, and our prayer was answered when a doctor in our church allowed us to rent his apartment in Wood Green, North London. However, when Jeannie was six months pregnant, he too decided to move back into his apartment.

It felt a bit like musical chairs, but we were so in love, we saw it as one big adventure.

God was teaching us to trust Him, and through it all, we had such peace in our hearts.

You will keep in perfect peace those whose minds are steadfast,
because they trust in you.

Isaiah 26:3

Again, we prayed and asked God to provide a home for us. This time, we wanted a home that we could stay in for more than just a few months. There was nothing available on the market in our budget, and we decided to apply for a council apartment (an apartment owned by the local council and rented at a reduced amount).

The demand for housing in London is always high, and several of our family and friends prayed as we went to the interview. Jeannie and I held hands and prayed as we waited for the decision. I will never forget what the lady said when she told us they were going to give us an apartment.

"I hope you realize, Mr. and Mrs. Long, you are jumping ahead of seven hundred people who have been waiting for a council apartment," she said.

The council accommodation was allocated on a points basis, and because Jeannie was pregnant and we were going to be homeless, we had a high score, and we jumped to the front on the queue!

We had such joy! We thanked God for answering our prayer. We had our first official home that was our very own! The apartment was in a bit of a rough neighborhood, but this was where God planted us, and we were going to serve and pray for our neighbors. The apartment was unfurnished, and we were grateful when a friend drove up to London with a truckload of secondhand furniture.

We made our home warm and cozy, and a few months later, Jeannie went in to labor. After nearly giving birth on the way to the Royal

Free Hospital due to rush hour traffic, our beautiful daughter Rebecca was born at 1:10 a.m. on January 22, 1982. After watching Jeannie being wheeled off to the ward with Rebecca nestled in beside her, I went back home, and weeping for joy, I thanked God for His love and the gift of our baby daughter.

They were such happy days. God's love filled our home, and many of our friends and family visited us. Our neighborhood may have been rough, our apartment was plain and filled with secondhand furniture, but we were rich in love and joy.

We were excited to welcome my mom, who was coming up to help Jeannie with our baby. The only problem was, I was in the middle of my banking exams, and I didn't have time to wallpaper our spare room. Instead, I found some pretty wrapping paper and decorated the area around her bed. Mom later told me that her heart was deeply touched by my efforts to make things as pretty as possible for her.

> *I have learned that:*
>
> *- there is a time when a young man launches into the unknown and has to trust God for His provision; and*
>
> *- quality of your life does not depend on external things but on what you have in your heart.*

29.

"I Am with You"

After my encounter with God in 1980, I committed my whole life to Him. That meant every part of my life. After praying, I decided to give away all my money, including my business. I wanted to start afresh and be totally dependent on the Lord.

As we trusted God, Jeannie and I saw the Lord graciously answer our prayers. This caused our faith to grow, and encouraged and inspired our hearts to trust that God was with us.

We were grateful for our small apartment, but it didn't have a garden. We prayed and asked God for our own home with a garden, and we both sensed God telling us that we would have one in two years.

We decided to write down what we wanted in our first house—a white double-fronted cottage-style house with a big garden (hard to find in London) and lots of flowers.

As a bank employee, I was entitled to a mortgage, but I had to raise the five percent deposit. That was a problem. Although I was on an executive management program, I was still not earning enough to cover our living expenses, let alone save for the deposit. In fact, we only got through each month because people in our small church gave us gifts. Some were anonymous, and at other times, people said something along the lines of, "God has told me to give you this money."

In line with His promise in Scripture, God was,

Meeting our needs according to his glorious riches in Christ Jesus.
Philippians 4:29

We never went without food, although at times things were very tight. On two occasions Jeannie didn't have any money in her purse, but each time an older woman came up to her, admired Rebecca, said something like "What a beautiful baby!" and pressed some money into Jeannie's hand (it's a tradition in London for older ladies to help young moms with some money). It was just enough for Jeannie to go to Chapel Street market and buy some vegetables and bread for a delicious soup for our evening meal.

As the two years came to an end, random people at the bank started telling me they thought it was time for us to buy our own home.

Rebecca's godmother rang to say she had a dream in which she saw me sitting on top of a house.

Jeannie's parents separated when her mother was pregnant with her, and she met her father for the first time when she was five years old. Although her father promised her many things, he never delivered. But suddenly, out of the blue, he said he was going to give us the money for a deposit for our house.

We were overjoyed that our prayers had been answered, and we were so excited to put our name down with several real estate agents. We received lists of houses, and in one batch, at the top of the first sheet was a white double-fronted cottage with a one-hundred-foot garden! The previous owners had been keen gardeners, and the garden was full of red, pink, yellow, and white rose bushes. When we saw it in person, the fragrance from the flowers filled the air.

Our faith grew as we saw how God had answered our prayers. He had given us everything we had asked for on our list. We were so grateful and so excited, and we gave thanks to God.

We bought the cottage. One of our new neighbors told us, "I knew this property was coming on the market, and I put in a bid. I thought it was going through, but at the last moment, it fell through. How did you manage to buy it?"

It was a fantastic opportunity to tell our new neighbor how we trusted God and how He had answered our special prayer.

It was awesome to think that from the beginning of time, God had planned the small, white double-fronted cottage for Jeannie and me.

We were so happy in our little cottage in Muswell Hill, North London. Ben and Alex were born while we were there. I had been promoted at the bank, and we were able to buy our first brand new item for our home.

Up to this point, all our household items had been given to us. But when my mother made some pretty curtains for our new cottage, we bought a brand-new wooden curtain pole. You can't imagine the fun that Jeannie and I had every time we looked at our new purchase. We laughed so much about the simplicity of our new household item and the joy it gave us.

I remembered my encounter with God at Loughborough and the revelation that in God we can find the greatest joy from the simplest of things.

> *I experienced that God's promises are true, and they can be trusted for our food and shelter, and everything else we need.*

I experienced that God answers specific prayers.

I experienced that we may not have many possessions in the world's eyes, yet we may be rich in terms of love, joy, and peace.

I experienced that without us knowing it, our lives can be a great witness to others.

Write down two of your prayers that have been answered and two that are still to be answered. There are so many simple things that bring color and joy to our lives, such as music, animals, flowers, and birds. What are the simple things you enjoy in life, and what can you do to make more time to let these things refresh your soul? What have you experienced in your life that has caused your faith to grow?

30.

Our Children

Jeannie and I were blessed with three wonderful children, Rebecca, Ben, and Alex. My heart was so full of love for Rebecca that when I found out Jeannie was pregnant again, I wondered how I could have that much love for our second child. When Ben was born, my heart seemed to grow, and I had the same love for him as I had for Rebecca. The same thing happened with Alex, too.

Our children are part of our lives and our future. I would love to introduce you to our children.

Rebecca

Rebecca was our honeymoon baby, and we were now a little family. We were in a state of bliss. I was so proud of Jeannie and Rebecca, and I couldn't wait to see them at the end of my workday. Suddenly, I was a new husband and a new dad, and I loved every minute of it.

From the beginning, Rebecca gave us so much joy. She was adventurous, eager, and curious.

As Rebecca grew up, she became more and more beautiful, both on the outside and on the inside. She was conscientious, intelligent, and popular, and she lived with an intensity to get on in life.

We were active in our church, and Rebecca often joined me when I visited people in the local council estates, much like the projects in the U.S. It was a special time together, and I could see Rebecca's tender heart being touched by the obvious pain and suffering we encountered among some of the families.

When she was 11, Rebecca asked if she could be baptized. Many of our family and friends attended, and the church was packed, with her best friends sitting on the front row. She gave her testimony, and a pastor, thinking she had finished, was about to move on to the next person when Rebecca said, "Oh, no! I have more to say." After sharing some more of her love for Jesus Christ, she ended with a song she felt the Lord had given her.

Like all parents, we wanted our daughter to attend a school that suited her personality and potential. After we prayed about it, Rebecca was selected for an excellent primary school on the top of Highgate Hill, close to where we lived in North London. The teaching and the culture of St. Michael's, a Church of England school, were exceptional.

Rebecca was an excellent student and was also the fastest runner in her school. In her final year at St. Michael's, she was spotted at the annual sports day and was invited to try out for Highgate Harriers, the main athletics club in our part of North London. How proud we all were when Rebecca won the 800-meter race, beating the best runners in the area! This was the start of Rebecca's running career.

In the UK, children move up to their senior or secondary school at 11 years old. We prayed with Rebecca about the next stage in her education. We were delighted when she was accepted to attend Francis Holland School, Regents Park, a leading Church of England school for girls. Rebecca loved the school and made several lifelong friends there.

Alongside her studies, Rebecca continued with her athletics. She was focused, disciplined, and courageous. She became a champion, winning the London schools 800 meters twice for her age group and representing London at the England Schools Championship.

After her senior school, Rebecca was accepted to Bristol University. Bristol is one of the top universities in the UK and had an excellent athletic program. Rebecca was delighted when she was awarded a place. She was soon running for their track team and was selected for the Elite Athlete squad.

She loved her time at Bristol University, and while starring on the track team, she got a degree in history.

Ben

Ben was born at the Royal Free Hospital, Hampstead Heath, on April 19, 1984. I had so much love for Ben that I wondered if I had grown a second heart.

Ben was demonstrative and loved to cuddle and be cuddled. He gave Jeannie and me so much joy, and he had a big sister who adored him.

From early on, we noticed how quick and intelligent Ben was. He had a big, kind, loving heart and would help anyone. As he grew up, he developed a great sense of humor and often made us laugh.

Ben came to faith in Christ. We noticed he had a love for God's Word and later enjoyed helping teach the youth group. We were overjoyed when Ben asked to be baptized.

Ben also attended St. Michael's School. He was popular and a great athlete, playing for the school soccer team.

We were so proud of Ben. At 11 years old, he passed the entrance exam for Queen Elizabeth Boys' School, Barnet. QE Boys, as it is known, is one of the top schools in London both for academics and sports. Only one in ten boys pass the entrance exam.

QE Boys was a big school with many talented athletes. It had one of the strongest rugby teams in London, and I was so proud of Ben when he was selected as fullback for his year's first team. We loved to watch Ben play, and we were all so delighted with his achievement. He was brave and courageous in the tackle, and he used his speed to run with the ball and take his team forward. I would usually lose my voice from shouting so hard for Ben and his team.

As well as excelling in rugby, Ben was also a good cross-country runner and ran for the school team. He too was selected for Highgate Harriers and competed on their cross-country and track teams.

Ben was an outstanding all-round athlete. He placed fourth in the South of England under 16 high-jump championship—in his first competition! He had the potential to be an excellent decathlete.

Alex

Alex, our youngest, was born almost four years after Ben, on December 13, 1987, at the Wittington Hospital, Archway. My heart grew again as I held my new baby son, and I loved him as I had Rebecca and Ben.

Alex was the baby of our family, and we all adored him. He completed our family.

Alex loved and looked up to his older brother and sister. Naturally, he wanted to do what they were doing, and this would often test their patience.

Alex came to faith in Christ as a young boy and developed a walk with the Lord. He had many friends at his church youth group. We could see Alex had a great heart for people, especially those who were struggling.

From an early age, we noticed that Alex had excellent eye-hand co-ordination and was outstanding at whatever ball game he played.

Alex also attended St. Michael's school. He was a fast runner, like his siblings. He won the sprint at the annual sports day and represented the school in soccer.

After St. Michael's, Alex qualified for a sports scholarship to an excellent private school in Elstree, just north of London. The smaller class sizes suited Alex. One of the masters told us that Alex had been identified as a potential future head boy. While at the school, Alex was selected to represent his school and county in field hockey and his school at football and cricket matches.

Of all his sporting talents, Alex's running ability caught my eye. He was incredibly gifted, and with strong legs and a long stride, he was fast and had good stamina. From a young age, like his brother and sister, Alex ran for Highgate Harriers.

By his mid-teens, it was clear to me that Alex had a rare and outstanding gift as a runner.

The most important thing for Jeannie and me was to bring our children up to know and love Jesus Christ. We thank God for answering our prayer; all our children came to faith in Christ at an early age.

I have learned that our children are a gift from the Lord, and they are only on loan to us. Treasure every moment you have with your children and make your time with them a priority.

31.

"His Grace Is Sufficient for Me"

Over the next few years, life was busy. As well as rearing our young family and my full-time job at the bank, I was also one of three pastors in our young and vibrant church. The church met on Sunday, and the rest of the week we did life together in our homes, meeting for meals, prayer, and special pastoral needs.

Sunday morning church was a special family time. I would normally preach once or twice a month. After church we usually invited a few people back for a Sunday roast. Jeannie would cook a roast chicken, together with roast potatoes, vegetables, and gravy, followed by a delicious dessert. After lunch we would walk in the park and play games.

On weekdays, I would cycle to work, leaving the house about 7:15 a.m. After work, I cycled hard, sometimes racing with other cyclists, eager to get home to see Jeannie and the children, to have tea together, to read bedtime stories, pray, and kiss the children good night. On some nights we had so much fun it was hard to get them off to sleep. On Monday nights, I met with the other two pastors for fellowship, prayer, worship, and planning. I would usually have meetings on at least two other nights of the week. Friday was reserved for Jeannie and me to have a special date night.

I learned many valuable lessons in this season of life. My most valuable lesson was a deeper understanding of God's grace and how it works in our lives.

My first priority was my personal time with God. It was in my time with Him that I received the grace for the day ahead. Often my body wanted to sleep on in the morning, but I knew that my inner strength came from my time with God. I would arise, make a nice cup of tea, and settle down at the kitchen table to give thanks, read the Bible, and pray.

> *I have learned that when I was in God's presence, my soul was being strengthened. What flowed from my time with God was love, strength, wisdom, joy, peace, and anything else I needed for the day ahead.*

Jeannie and I often reminded each other of this inspiring Scripture:

> *But those who wait on the LORD*
> *Shall renew their strength;*
> *They shall mount up with wings like eagles,*
> *They shall run and not be weary,*
> *They shall walk and not faint.*

Isaiah 40:31

> *I have learned that the time of day and the length of time I spend with God is not as important as my heart wanting to connect with Him!*

The Lord taught me that the length and the width and the height and the depth of His grace are immeasurably more than I can imagine.

I have learned that God's grace is the life of Jesus made known to me by the Holy Spirit (John 16:14).

His grace saved my soul and equips me with everything I need to do His will (Ephesians 2:8, Hebrews 13:20-21).

At this time in my life, I particularly needed physical strength and wisdom to care for my family, to help lead the church, and do an excellent job at work. And this is what God gave me.

In Him we live and move and have our being.

Acts 17:28

I have learned a bit more about God's grace—His love and provision, given to us in Jesus.

32.

Faith in the Workplace

Corporate life can be a cutthroat environment. I asked the Lord to give me the strength and wisdom to be true to my beliefs and my commitment to Him. I would search out one of God's promises for whatever I was going through, and Jeannie and I both felt the following Scripture was an anchor to hold on to in the challenges of the workplace:

Seek first His kingdom and His righteousness, and all these things will be given to you as well.

Matthew 6:33

There were many things that pulled against my love for God and seeking His kingdom. It was a daily challenge to hold to my faith and to keep my heart from being diluted in my commitment to Him.

I prayed and asked God for opportunities to share my faith with my work colleagues. Early in my banking career, the opportunities were few and far between. In one office, I worked for four years before an opening came. My colleagues knew I was a Christian, but I had never had the opportunity to share my faith. One day, a door opened for me. We were all chatting, and out of the blue, someone asked me, "Gerard, what does your Christian faith mean to you?" It was a God moment. After watching me for years, my colleagues were attentive as I spent ten minutes or so sharing my testimony and the good news about Jesus Christ.

> *I have learned that people do take note of how Christians live their lives, and our actions and attitudes are often more powerful than our words.*

I had read in the Bible that God would test my heart as He prepared me for the work He had planned for me in this age and in the age to come. I was about to have one of the biggest tests we all face: Did I fear man more than I loved and trusted God?

> *The fear of the LORD is the beginning of wisdom.*
> **Proverbs 9:10**

Interestingly, the middle verse of the Bible, says:

> *It is better to trust in the LORD than to put confidence in man.*
> **Psalm 118:8**

I had a season when God put me face-to-face with the Giant of Fear—my name for Satan's attempts to stop me from progressing in my Christian faith—which tried to control my life.

I was promoted to work on a small corporate planning team that supported various senior executives in the head office. Our office was one floor below the executives, and every now and again, I was called to deliver a report or some information to them. The carpet on the executive floor was about an inch thick, and the walls were lined with portraits of past chairmen. The executives all had their own plush offices and one or more personal assistants.

I was humbled to be working in such a prestigious environment. I highly respected the executives.

Everything was fine until I sensed that God wanted me to start wearing a fish emblem on the lapel of my suit. A fish emblem was first used by the early Christians as a secret sign to identify each other during the Roman persecution. The Greek letters for " fish" form an acronym for "Jesus Christ, Son of God, Savior."

The Giant of Fear stood in front of me, and for several weeks, I struggled putting on the fish emblem. I heard the Giant of Fear whispering in my ear, "What will they think of you? You're going to be labeled a fanatical Christian. This is going to be the end of your banking career. How will you be able to care for your family when you lose your job?"

Wearing my fish emblem, and with my heart pounding, I knocked on the executive's door.

I heard a voice call out, "Come in," and with my adrenalin pumping, I stepped into the office. Much to my relief, the executive made me feel welcome. I don't think he even noticed my fish emblem. When I think about it now, I wonder what all the fuss was about! But at the time, it was a real struggle.

We can all face Giants of Fear that try to prevent us from moving forward in our faith, and often it has to do with the fear of man or the fear of the future.

The question I had to answer was, "Do I believe and trust in the Word of God, or am I going to listen to the Giant of Fear?" Faith and fear cannot live together.

I have learned that this is how God tests my heart. He leads me into challenging situations to give me the opportunity to learn that His Word is true, and it can be trusted!

This is how God led the children of Israel through the wilderness and into the promises He had given them:

Remember how the LORD your God led you all the way in the wilderness these forty years, to humble and test you in order to know what was in your heart, whether or not you would keep his commands. He humbled you, causing you to hunger and then feeding you with manna, which neither you nor your ancestors had known, to teach you that man does not live on bread alone but on every word that comes from the mouth of the LORD.

Deuteronomy 8:2-3

With a lot of prayer, and after several weeks of struggle, God's grace enabled me to triumph over the Giant of Fear. Since that battle, I've been eager for an opportunity to share my faith at work or wherever I am.

I have learned that faith and my struggles often go together, and I need to persevere until God brings me into victory.

That's not to say I have taken every opportunity I've had. On the contrary, I know I've missed countless chances to share my faith, and I thank God for His mercy and grace to give me many more chances.

A friend of mine told me of his own experience of wearing a fish emblem. He was in a high-profile situation and was standing in a group of influential people. Suddenly, one of the guys turned to my friend and asked, "Tell me, what does that fish emblem mean that you're wearing?" His heart was racing as all eyes turned toward him, and in a moment of panic, he answered, "Oh, it means, 'Save the Whales!'"

Like the Apostle Peter, he recovered from his denial of Christ. He's one of the godliest men I've ever known.

> *I have learned that:*
>
> *- God's promises can be trusted in the workplace, and it's better to trust God than to fear man; and*
>
> *- to make my faith real to me, it must be tested in the furnace of affliction.*

How is your faith being tested at the moment?

Season Six—Harvest Time

I love the seasons. In England, there are usually three months each for summer, autumn, winter, and spring. There is something special about each season, the long summer days at the beach or walking in the countryside, the changing colors of autumn, the cozy open fires in winter, and the abundance of new life and harvest in the spring. I have to say, with the colors and aroma of the flowers and blossoms, spring is my favorite season.

> *I have learned that there are parallels between my life and the seasons.*

There are times when everything is running smoothly, and I'm enjoying life. It's a summer season. But then, I face some challenges, and things that used to work, no longer run so smoothly. Parts of my life seem to be falling apart; an autumn season. And, there are times when life is especially hard. Every step is a struggle, and God seems so distant. My heart seems to be wintery cold! But then, it's springtime again, and all the things that I thought were dead start to produce new life.

> *I have learned that the deeper my roots of faith go into God's Word, the more faithful I am in my witness for Christ, even during a winter season.*

In the next few chapters, I am going to tell you about a spring season in my life—a time of harvest, when whatever I put my hand to, produced great fruit.

> *I have learned that God is closer to me in my times of brokenness than in my times of abundance. His hand of blessing is on me as much in a winter season as in the harvest of springtime.*

33.

Harvest in the City

I met Mike at a church service in the City. In many ways, Mike and I were different, but we had one thing in common. We both loved Jesus Christ and wanted to share with our colleagues the love, truth, and eternal life we had experienced in Him.

We decided to follow Jesus' teaching to pray together. We kept it simple. On one day of the week, we got into work half an hour earlier than normal, found an empty conference room, and prayed for God's kingdom to come and for His will to be done in our workplace, *as it is in heaven* (Matthew 6:10).

Yes, the Giant of Fear turned up again and tried to stop us by saying, "If your colleagues find out what you're doing, you will be ridiculed, and you may lose your job." He had forgotten he was already defeated, and he didn't stay for long.

Other Christians started to join us, and emboldened, we decided to take a courageous step. We put a message in the bank's head of office circular inviting Christians to join us in prayer. Of course, some people said we'd never be able to do it and that no one would respond. Whenever you step out in faith, there is usually opposition, but God uses this to test and strengthen our faith.

We were shocked by the response to our public invitation. More than a hundred people contacted us, and within a few weeks, there were six separate prayer meetings taking place in different head office buildings across the City.

People started to come to faith in Christ, and some of the senior executives got involved. Other banks started prayer gatherings, and many joined in the midweek praise, worship, and outreach meetings at St. Margaret's Church, Lothbury.

At one of the St. Margaret's invitation meetings, I was asked to follow up on a man named John. John worked in the same bank as me, but after looking through all the telephone directories, I couldn't track him down.

"Oh, Lord!" I prayed, "please help me find John."

Several days later, I was surprised when someone rang me and asked, "Is that John H—?" It turned out that out of thousands of employees in the City, John and I had similar five-digit internal numbers, and the caller had mistyped the number! "No," I said. "I'm not John H—, but I am trying to find him. Do you know where he works?"

John had the job of a Messenger in a nearby building. On a lunch break, I went to meet John and he was surprised when I told him how I had found him.

"John," I said, "it's no coincidence that I was able to find you. God cares about you, and He clearly helped me to find you."

John was going through a hard time, and he was grateful that I made the effort to meet him. He later came to faith in Christ. The Lord helped him in his troubles, and we became friends.

I have learned that:

- if God can move in the City, the financial center of Europe, He can move in any workplace and any industry ; and

- I need to stand up to the Giant of Fear and step out and affirm my faith, to share God's love and the good news of Jesus Christ, in my family, workplace, neighborhood, and wherever God has planted me.

I am so inspired by the early Christians who, being filled with the Holy Spirit, turned the world upside down (Acts 17:6).

On being threatened not to speak about Jesus, they answered:

Which is right in God's eyes: to listen to you, or to Him?
You be the judges! As for us, we cannot help speaking about what we have seen and heard.

Acts 4:19-20

Somehow, stepping out in faith releases God's power and His kingdom. Abraham is one of my heroes in the Bible. I love how he walked by faith:

You see that his faith and his actions were working together, and his faith was made complete by what he did.

James 2:22

From the early 1990s, I led "Christians in Finance," a group that was formed in the 1800s. We met every Friday at lunchtime at St. Margaret's for fellowship, worship, Bible study, and outreach. We also prayed at St. Margaret's for an hour before work on a Thursday or Friday morning.

In the late 1990s, we started to run Alpha, a six-week course introducing people to Jesus Christ, in the workplace. We met at lunchtime at the bank, at Lloyds Insurance, and after work at St. Margaret's.

> *I have learned that nothing is too hard for the Lord when we step out in faith; God can make a way when there seems to be no way.*

34.

Harvest in the Neighborhood

Our little white double-fronted cottage could well have been in a country village. It was exactly what we had prayed for! We thanked God for our new home and I loved our time there.

Rebecca and Ben attended the local school and Jeannie started a ballet school. I started a football team for our church as a way to connect with the men in the neighborhood.

We made many new friends and always prayed that the love and presence of the Lord would be experienced in our home. We were encouraged when God started to touch their lives.

John and Sarah were the parents of one of Rebecca's friends. Over a coffee, Jeannie was encouraged when Sarah suddenly mentioned how inspired she was to meet such a happy family. We later learned that Sarah was very house proud and she thought that material possessions brought happiness. She had been surprised by the love and peace we had, even though our house was at its humble beginnings. Jeannie had a wonderful opportunity to share how her faith in Jesus had shown her the true meaning of life. A short time later, Sarah came to faith in Christ, but she was convinced her husband, John, would never believe.

I made friends with John, who was quite a character. I invited him to be the goalkeeper for our church football team. During one match, John was surprised to hear the supporters singing Christian songs behind his goal. After the match, John shared with me his surprise, because on all the other teams he had played for, all he ever heard was cursing. We spent time with John and Sarah and in answer to our prayers, and to Sarah's surprise, John also came to faith in Christ. We invited the whole family to church and I will never forget the smile on John's face when he told me how surprised he was one Sunday morning when someone taught from the book of Job, and he was praying for a new job! I laughed along with John but decided not to say anything about how the book of Job was pronounced.

We were excited when two couples from our church decided to move into the neighborhood. Stan and Christine purchased the cottage next door to us. We became friends, and one day, in tears, they told us about something that was troubling them. They had been trying to have a baby for several years. They asked us to pray for them, and nine months later, we thanked God for a wonderful answer to prayer—they were blessed with a baby boy! Believe it or not, shortly after, we were asked to pray for another couple who had been trying to have a baby for seven years. Miraculously, God answered this prayer too. Oh! How we rejoiced together at the birth of their son the following year!

Bernard and Connie were the other couple who purchased a house in the neighborhood. They became very dear friends, and we did life together. To this day, they have remained among our closest friends.

To get to work, I would drive to the nearest railway station. When our old car died on us, we prayed for another car, and received an encouraging answer. Someone from our church gave us a car. The only problem was, the car was difficult to start in the morning. Jeannie and the children would stand at the window praying, while I tried to round up neighbors to give me a push-start.

Rebecca and Ben thought this was great fun and would cheer and thank God when they saw me driving off. As long as I parked on a hill, I would be good for getting back in the evening. Our friends thought all this was amusing and nicknamed our car "Yellow Peril."

After six years, we sensed God was calling us to move to be nearer our church in Kentish Town. Our friends and neighbors didn't want us to go but the call from God was clear and we wanted to be obedient.

Most young families usually move out of London for better housing and better schools. It would be a leap of faith for us, because house prices were much higher the closer we got to central London. We looked to God to provide, trusting that He would guide us as we started our search for another home.

We looked at a house on Chetwynd Road, Dartmouth Park, that was around the corner from where our church met. We loved the house, but the price was way too high for us. Jeannie and I prayed and left the house in God's hands. A few months later, we received a phone call from the real estate agent. The owners hadn't been able to sell their house, and they wanted to know if we were still interested. This time, they were offering it at the exact price we could afford.

Once again, God was making a way when there seemed to be no way. We sold our Muswell Hill home for four times what we paid for it and moved into a four-bedroom terrace house in Dartmouth Park. It would be our home for the next 10 years. During that time, God blessed us in so many wonderful ways.

> *I have learned that:*
>
> *- if you seek God's will first, all the other things naturally follow;*
>
> *- it's not so much the splendor of our possessions that touch people but the life flowing from within;*

- *God loves to reach the most unlikely people; and*

- *in His time and His will, God will open doors that appear to be closed.*

35.

Harvest in the Church

We settled in to our new home in Dartmouth Park, and it felt so good to be near where our church met in the local school.

Our church was called New Life Christian Fellowship (NLCF). It was a young, nondenominational church, and Rebecca had been the first of many babies there.

Prayer was central to everything we did at NLCF. We emphasized the importance of prayer for individuals, home groups, pastors, and whatever we did. Sometimes we would have seasons of fasting and half-nights of prayer.

Shortly after we moved, our church experienced a harvest time, as a lot of people came to faith in Christ. Let me tell you how this came about and how Steve was converted and baptized.

On a pastor's weekend of prayer and seeking the Lord, we felt God speaking to us about changing the structure and focus of the church. From being mainly inward-looking, God called us to reach out to our neighborhood.

We did all sorts of things, from running youth clubs, summer camps on Hampstead Heath, praise marches through Camden and Kentish Town, outreach in pubs, Christmas carols, door-to-door activities, and even an annual sports day. It was hard work, but it was also exciting and lots of fun to see God moving through the church. We saw people come to faith in Christ. In one of our door-to-door activities, a young couple who were Jehovah's Witnesses received Christ and joined the small group we were holding in our home.

In 1995, we started running Alpha in our home, and we ran it for the next five years, three times a year. Although it was hard work, and Jeannie had her hands full with feeding the children, preparing the home, and getting the food ready for our guests, it was great fun. It was a powerful experience and a privilege to witness drug addicts, prostitutes, gang members, and other colorful characters being transformed before our eyes as they received Jesus Christ as their Lord and Savior.

We had several exciting Alpha groups. One I particularly remember was nearly all men, including a communist from the Czech Republic and two drug addicts. One of the addicts was a guy named Steve. He had arrived at our home on the opening evening of Alpha.

I have to admit, when I opened the door to Steve, I was a little concerned about letting him into our home. Steve seemed to be angry and hostile, and at six feet three inches tall, he was a little intimidating! Over the weeks, I got to know Steve, and I understood why he was angry. After a dysfunctional childhood, Steve became a drug addict, gang member, and street fighter. He had also been afflicted with terrible depression for seven years and hadn't worked for five years.

Alpha starts with a meal, followed by a talk covering the teachings of Jesus, and ends with a discussion, in which the guests are encouraged to raise any questions or concerns about what they had just heard, although they often raise other issues as well.

Most of the group did not believe in Christ. We had a number of contentious discussion times, often started by Steve.

Thankfully, we all survived the ten-week course without anyone coming to blows, and we were surprised and delighted when the communist and the two drug addicts asked if they could do the course again.

During Steve's second Alpha course, I invited him to come to church. The next Sunday I was leading the service and was overjoyed when I saw Steve come in and seat himself at the back. I was even more pleased when, at the end of the service, Steve responded to my invitation for anyone who wanted prayer. I asked him if I could lay my hand on him as I prayed for him. He agreed, and as I began to pray, God touched Steve, and he started to sob from the bottom of his heart. I'll never forget the pool of tears around Steve's feet. That morning, years of hurt and pain were lifted off Steve, as he received Jesus Christ as his Lord and Savior!

The next morning, Steve woke up and was completely healed of depression. He rang his mother and said, "Mom, I'm healed!" The next day, he got a job, and the following week, he was promoted to manager of his telephone sales team.

Steve was later baptized along with the communist guy and the other drug addict. What a great celebration we had! There must have been an even bigger one in heaven!

I later asked Steve, "Why did you keep on coming back to Alpha, when you were so aggressive during the first course?"

"Oh," said Steve, "it was because you never judged me."

Jeannie and I loved the twenty-two years we served as part of NLCF, and in all our travels, we've never found a church like it. We still consider it our home church in the UK.

> *I experienced how much God is concerned about every individual. No one is beyond His love and grace.*

36.

Harvest at Work

It was harvest time for me in the workplace. I was seeing God move in many wonderful ways. I had a chat with a janitor one morning, and he told me how worried he was because his wife was sick. I asked him if I could pray for his wife. He was grateful and I said a simple prayer for his sick wife. He later told me that his wife started to get better about the time we prayed. Not everyone I prayed for in the workplace was healed, but some were.

All through my banking career, as I held to my priority to see God's kingdom come in my workplace, I kept getting promoted. I never applied or pushed for promotion. I knew the promotions were coming from the Lord.

One promotion came after I received a prophetic word from a lady in our church.

Judy had grown up in Kentish Town. She used to be very tough and certainly not someone you'd want to cross. After she came to faith in Jesus Christ, God poured His love into her heart by the Holy Spirit (Romans 5:5), and she became a different person. Whenever I saw her, she seemed to have an aura of peace and joy around her, even though she still had challenges in her life.

One Sunday after the morning service, Judy came up to Jeannie and me and told us she felt she had a word from the Lord for me. She said she had a vision of me standing on a stage with a spotlight on me. At the time, none of us knew what it meant.

People were coming to faith at work, but I had been going through a challenging time. I had a difficult boss, and for some reason, she had it in for me.

Working late one night, I said to a close Christian friend, "I'm not sure what God is doing, but I'm finding it so hard with my boss." With tears in my eyes, I said, "But I believe this is where God wants me at this time."

Whenever I'm going through a hard time, Jeannie and I take it to the Lord in prayer and ask others to pray too. One of the most powerful spiritual disciplines I do is to memorize Scripture. When I'm going through a hard time, the Holy Spirit reminds me of a Scripture that will inspire and encourage me in my trial. The Scripture that came to mind at the time was Psalm 27:5:

For in the day of trouble He will keep me safe in his dwelling; He will hide me in the shelter of his sacred tent and set me high upon a rock.

I have learned how powerful God's Word is, and I strongly encourage you to develop a habit of memorizing Scripture.

The next day, I received a phone call from the head office, and I was asked to consider a job running the bank's Year 2000 program. Y2K, or the millennium bug, was a global problem that threatened to impact computer code and microchips that had a coding flaw that would be activated when the calendar rolled to the year 2000.

This turned out to be the biggest and most influential promotion I ever received at the bank. It was as though I was actually living the words in Psalm 27:6, which says:

Then my head will be exalted above the enemies who surround me; at His sacred tent I will sacrifice with shouts of joy; I will sing and make music to the LORD.

The role turned out to be bigger than anyone could have imagined. Very quickly, my head was exalted above my former boss, who had caused me so much trouble.

Midland Bank was acquired by Hongkong and Shanghai Banking Corporation (HSBC). I was promoted to senior manager and put in charge of HSBC's preparation for resolving the millennium bug. It was my responsibility to ensure the bank had every line of code, microchip, corporate customer, and the business as a whole prepared and ready for when time clicked into the new millennium.

It was 1997, and the more I looked into the problem, the bigger the challenge was. We had to get moving.

Because of what is known as just-in-time processing, one failure of computer code or a microchip could break a whole supply chain and potentially close a factory and put thousands of people out of work.

Time was running out, and a head of state needed to highlight how serious the issue was. We contacted government officials, and I visited 10 Downing Street several times to plan for the Prime Minister, Tony Blair, to speak at the HSBC conference.

The conference was held in a large auditorium in the Barbican. I met the Prime Minister at his car, and together with his security team, escorted him up to the huge auditorium. Unfortunately, one of the security guys pressed the button for the wrong floor on the elevator.

The door opened. I will never forget the look on the face of the janitor—mop in hand and cigarette hanging from her mouth—as her morning was interrupted by a chance meeting with the Prime Minister!

Our conference was broadcast on prime-time TV on all the main UK channels and around the world. After the conference, everything seemed to happen so fast. I was asked to give expert advice on the Y2K problem on TV, radio, and other media. I was even quoted on the front page of USA Today!

Jeannie and I never stopped thanking God for my promotion. Through it all, I was encouraged by Judy's prophecy. All the great favor and influence I had been given inside and outside of the bank was God's blessing—part of the time of harvest!

I was in the HSBC control and command center overnight on December 31, 1999. My team had worked so hard, and I had asked many people to pray. As the clocks clicked over to the year 2000, I was confident we were all going to be okay. Nothing dire happened, and Jeannie and I thanked God for His grace, enabling me to play a key role in this major initiative.

Later, the governor of the Bank of England thanked us for the work we had done to avert what could have been a catastrophe. As a "thank you" from HSBC, Jeannie and I were sent on an all-expenses-paid skiing trip to Whistler, Canada. We had a fantastic time, and after a gap of 26 years, I renewed my love for skiing. Jeannie was pleased for me, but she became concerned when she heard that I had joined a group of men with ponytails, who were skiing off piste—off the marked trails!

I have learned that:

- God can suddenly change my situation, but I have to trust Him for the timing;

- the Lord can promote me to a high position at any time; and

- I need to walk by faith and make sure fear doesn't keep me from my purpose.

Scripture teaches us to remember God's grace and His acts of lovingkindness. Can you remember challenges at home or in the workplace, in which God gave you the grace to overcome and resolve the issues? When you remember how God helped you in the past, how does that make you feel about any challenges you may face in the future?

37.

Harvest in France

The recognition I received for the Year 2000 role led to my selection for a prestigious international executive management course in France. The course was for potential captains of industry from all around the world and included young executives from various Fortune 500 companies, such as Tata Steel, L'Oréal, and Fiat. It was held at the European Centre for Executive Development (CEDEP) located on the campus of INSEAD, a graduate business school in Fontainebleau, about 50 km from Paris.

I was grateful to be selected for the course, but I was reluctant to attend because it meant being away from Jeannie and the family for nine weeks—four two-week periods and one week at the end. The first session was challenging, because I felt intense spiritual opposition. I asked Jeannie and several close friends and family to pray, and I strengthened myself in God's Word by meditating on various Scriptures. From then on, there was a noticeable paradigm shift in the atmosphere, and my time at CEDEP was a lot easier. I made some new friends, and I had several opportunities to share my faith.

In the penultimate session, we covered public speaking. We were split into five groups of 12 people, and each person was videotaped speaking in front of the group on a topic they were passionate about.

I knew there was only one thing I was passionate about, and that was my love for Christ. Yes, the Giant of Fear turned up again with all sorts of excuses, including the fact the attendees were young executives from influential corporations around the world. I wondered what they would think of me. But I wanted to be true to my heart, and I knew I would feel terrible if I missed this opportunity to witness to my colleagues.

And so, with my heart racing, I stood in front of my group and spoke about my faith and love for Jesus Christ. There is a strong atheist spirit in Europe, and I could see on my colleagues' faces that what I was saying was having an impact. After we had all spoken, the lecturers critiqued each of our presentations from the video recording, and the group picked one speaker they wanted to go forward to the main group. To my shock, they asked me to present my story to the larger group.

In front of sixty or so potential future captains of industry, I was able to tell them the good news of Jesus Christ. I wish I could have taken a picture of some of the faces as I spoke.

Seeds of life were sown that day in people who might never get another opportunity to hear the gospel. I thanked God for the door He opened for me. My presentation was voted in the top two, and it triggered some great conversations during our remaining time together.

> *I learned that God can provide opportunities to witness for Him in the most unexpected places, even in an overseas executive management course.*

38.

Harvest in America

After the Year 2000 job, I had great favor within the bank, and I was promoted to head up a major branch network development initiative.

Around this time, Jeannie and I both started to have a stirring in our hearts. This didn't make any sense, because life was good. One lunchtime when I was walking through London, I prayed, "Lord, thank You for the blessings in my life, but please show me why I'm sensing this stirring inside. I just want to know Your will."

The stirring continued, and the hunger to know God's will increased, but we still didn't know what God had for us.

At the beginning of 2001, we invited a well-known speaker to our church. The lady had a prophetic gift. She prayed over all three of the pastors and their wives. For me, she said, "The Lord is going to send you overseas to lead missionary teams."

We taught that a prophetic word needed to be discerned and tested against scripture. After the service, I said to Jeannie, "Well, she got that one wrong, didn't she?" Although we were sensing a change was coming, we couldn't imagine going overseas.

Jeannie and I believed our calling was to serve God in London until He returned or we went home to heaven.

The stirring continued. Jeannie and I, together with some close friends, prayed and asked God for direction. After praying, we believed God was leading us to sell our house and to start renting a home. It was hard to leave our home, but as it turned out, God was freeing us up for a major change in our lives.

Then, in August, the chief operating officer of the bank called me into his big, plush office.

"Gerard," he said, "we have an excellent next role for you. We want you to go to New York to help launch a new and exciting global initiative."

As politely as I could, I answered, "David, it sounds interesting, and I'm honored that you should consider me for the role. The thing is, Jeannie and I would prefer to stay in London. We have so many commitments here, including the children's schooling and our church."

"That's a shame," David replied, and I could hear the disappointment in his voice. "This is a great opportunity for you and your career in the bank. It's your choice, and if you want to stay in London we'll find a job for you here. Before you make your decision, I want you to discuss the opportunity with Jeannie and let me know your answer in 48 hours."

As I left David's office, I knew I needed to hear God's voice. Was this offer connected to the stirring we had been sensing? And what about the prophetic word the lady had spoken over me earlier that year? My mind whirled. It would be a huge upheaval for Jeannie and the children. And what about all our friends and family? We had helped to build our church over the last 22 years, and we loved every member. In London, God was moving in countless ways. Would He move us on when we were helping to lead various initiatives? I thought of how God sent Philip on a mission while great things were going on in Jerusalem. I realized that the only thing that mattered was knowing if this was God's will for us.

I quickly asked trusted family and friends for their prayers and advice, and surprisingly, everyone, including Jeannie and the children, believed God was in this major move. On the day of decision, I said to Jeannie, "Darling, I still think I should turn down the bank's offer." The night before, I had been at a church meeting and didn't get a chance to talk with her about it one last time.

"Your mother rang last night," Jeannie said, "and she had a word for you. It was from Genesis chapter 24, when Rebekah was willing to go to a foreign land to be Isaacs's wife. She didn't tarry."

We knew my mother didn't want us to leave the UK, but she was being obedient to pass on what God had shown her.

This was my tipping point. We decided to accept the new role and go to America. Like Gideon, in the Bible, who asked God to confirm His instructions with a sign, we put out a fleece and asked the Lord for a sign.

Normally, I biked to work, but because I was running Alpha that night in a pub in Camden, I took the tube—the underground subway—into work. It was rare for me to meet anyone I knew on the tube, but that morning, I bumped straight into a guy I had met the week before, who told me he had worked for five years in Manhattan.

After work, I caught the Northern line at Bank station, where thousands of commuters were racing to get home. As I squeezed into the train, I bumped straight into a guy who was attending our Alpha course. The course only had about thirty people, but this guy had also worked in Manhattan.

The chance of meeting a person I knew on both journeys was highly unlikely.

The fact they had both worked in Manhattan was remarkable. And that this happened on the day I was accepting the job in Manhattan was almost unbelievable! I was so encouraged. Yes, the upcoming move was going to be heartwrenching, but God had confirmed our calling to America!

I have learned that:

- in decisions: God's peace leads me along the path He has planned for me;

- when God has planned a change in my life, He is able to arrange circumstances to bring it about;

- even when things are going well, God may still be calling me to another assignment; and

- my job is to keep my heart soft before Him and not to fret.

Above all else, guard your heart,
for everything you do flows from it.

Proverbs 4:23

39.

A New Adventure

We had many emotional farewell parties with our family and friends, and we found it particularly hard to say goodbye to our parents and our church family of the last 22 years. Through the tears and hugs, we left the shores of England for a new adventure in America.

It was an exhausting time, but we were also excited for what lay ahead. After prayer and viewing several houses in Rye, New York, we finally chose a contemporary house, with a peaceful view across the water toward Long Island Sound. In keeping with the nautical setting, the house was built in the shape of a boat; later we learned it had won an award for its design.

The best thing about our time in Rye was the friends we made. Before we left England, a friend gave us a list of people who could help us settle in to our new life. For a bit of fun, I picked out two names from the list and asked Jeannie to do the same. Independently, we both picked a couple named Bill and Jami.

Shortly after arriving in America, Bill picked us up at Rye train station and treated us to a delicious lunch of fresh rolls with lashings of delicious beef, chicken, and salad. The quantity and quality of the food gave us our first experience of American portions. It was a contrast to what we had been used to in the UK, and it would take me some time to learn that it was acceptable to not eat every last crumb.

I liked Bill and I felt he had a good heart and that he was a man of great integrity.

"I think you're going to get on with Jami," Bill told Jeannie. When they met, their hearts bonded in their love for Jesus. Jami has endless energy, and as well as being a great mom to her five children, she was involved in several women's Bible studies and prayer meetings. Jami and Jeannie became great friends. When Rebecca visited from the UK, she looked after their children when Bill and Jami were traveling.

Alex became friends with Bill and Jami's oldest son, Hank. They attended a fantastic Christian summer camp together, and Alex came home with stories of all the fun they had camping next to a lake.

Over the years, Bill and Jami have become more like family than friends. They are two of the most generous people you could meet, and they have shown us wonderful love and kindness over the years.

We enjoyed our time in Rye. In the snowy winters, we looked forward to the weekends when we headed off to the mountains to ski. In the summer, I loved to play golf, and it just so happened that our house was next to a golf course.

40.

Changes

The move to America was a big change for Rebecca, Ben, and Alex. They were so courageous in embracing it.

Rebecca was still at Bristol University finishing her history degree, but we were all excited at the thought of meeting up for Christmas and other vacations.

After Rebecca graduated, she decided to stay in London to focus on her running, training with her coach at Highgate Harriers. Although we all missed each other, Rebecca's hard work and training paid off when she was selected to represent Middlesex County at the South of England championships.

Ben was at QE Boys when we moved to America, studying for important exams for university entrance. He stayed six more months to finish his exams and then joined us in America. He was accepted for his senior year at Rye Country Day School and with his good looks and English accent, Ben was an immediate hit with the girls.

After his first day at Rye Country Day, Ben said to Jeannie, "Wow, if my friends could see me now, they'd think I was in heaven."

Ben is gregarious, has a great sense of humor, and he settled in well.

He made many new friends. Some even asked for coaching on how to speak with an English accent.

He enjoyed his year at Rye Country Day School, and with his height and speed, Ben was an excellent addition to their soccer team. It came as a great surprise to him at the end of the year when he was voted the prom king and had to dance with the prom queen.

Ben is naturally bright and achieved an excellent SAT score, which, together with his qualifications from the UK and a brilliant interview, landed him a place at Loughborough University. I was so proud that Ben accepted the offer to attend my old university. He would have a great opportunity to develop his natural athletic abilities, especially in the high jump.

Alex was in middle school when we moved to America. He worked hard at the American exams and had a good interview for a place at the Masters School in Dobbs Ferry, N.Y. At the end of the school year, Alex was asked to give a speech on what it meant to move from England to America, and we were moved to tears as he shared his thoughts.

With his natural athletic ability, he was delighted to be selected for all the sports teams. Playing lacrosse for the first time, I laughed when Alex came home with the comment, "Wow, in lacrosse you're allowed to hit each other."

I was so proud of how Rebecca, Ben, and Alex bravely tackled the changes and the challenges they faced in our move to America. Jeannie and I thanked God for our children and for our new adventure.

41.

Fifth Avenue

I commuted to work by train from Rye to Grand Central and walked five minutes, arriving at work around 8:00 a.m. It was such a contrast from biking to work in London. I had to pinch myself as I gazed out the window at the people playing basketball and the American flags blowing in the wind. It was only a few months after 9/11, and seeing the stars and stripes touched my heart, because they represented our determination to triumph over terrorism.

I'm not one to use the word surreal, but it truly was surreal to walk through Grand Central Station, which I had seen in films, and to take in the new smells of hot dogs and fresh coffee.

I felt proud to walk into HSBC's plush head office at Fifth Avenue and 40th Street. My office was on the eighth floor, and I was part of a small, select team working to launch an exciting new global product.

I settled in to my new routine. A highlight for me was when Jeannie joined me for lunch in Bryant Park, just across from my office. Jeannie and Alex did so well adjusting to their new life in America, and although they had some challenges, they quickly settled down.

But for the first six months, I struggled. I had more than I could have imagined on the outside, but on the inside, I lost my peace. My heart was longing to see God's kingdom come to pass, and I started running Alpha in the bank's boardroom. Apart from this, I had little or no other church responsibilities, and compared to all that I had been doing in London, it seemed as though I had been sidelined.

It was another battle of faith. Was I going to trust that God had led us to America and that He was behind this new season of great blessing and prosperity?

Jeannie was patient with me as I worked things through, and God's mercy and grace came to my rescue. The lies of Satan were exposed and, once again, I enjoyed my walk with God in the abundant life He had given me.

After I completed my initial assignment, the bank gave me another promotion—to manage the integration of HSBC's $13.8 billion acquisition of Household International.

I reported to the HSBC group IT director, and when he returned to London, he gave me his office overlooking Fifth Avenue. Several friends and acquaintances visited me in my new office, and some commented on the favor I had been given.

As the integration progressed, I needed to be based in Household's head office in Chicago. Jeannie and I discussed and prayed about me commuting to Chicago, but in the end we decided we should move to be nearer my workplace.

It was going to be another major upheaval for the family.

A big prayer request was to find a new school for Alex. Jeannie and I usually found it relatively easy to agree on things, but this was different. We disagreed on what would be the best school for Alex, and later, when the darkness came, it provoked some painful conversations.

We looked at several schools in the area and finally picked Loyola Academy, Wilmette, Illinois.

I wanted Alex to have the opportunity to develop his outstanding running ability, and I felt Loyola would give him the best chance to do this. It wasn't long before his talent was spotted, and as a sophomore, he was selected to run varsity 400 meters. With little training, Alex ran 400 meters at around 50 seconds and won the school prize as the most talented athlete.

Of course, I'm biased, but with his background in cross-country and his tall, lean but powerful physique, I knew he had the potential to get to the top in athletics as an 800-meter runner. We worked with Alex's coaches for a sports scholarship to college, but tragically, we were never going to watch Alex blossom into his full potential in running or anything else.

Working with a real estate agent, Jeannie looked at several potential homes across the North Shore of Chicago. Eventually, we settled on a house in Lake Forest, a suburb of Chicago.

Shortly after the move to Chicago, we were delighted to hear that Rebecca had been offered a running scholarship to earn an MBA at Loyola University in Chicago. She became a star on their track team, and while she was there, held the league record for 800 meters. We were overjoyed when Rebecca decided to live with us while she was in Chicago.

Life was good, very good. It was a season of abundance in every area of my life—my walk with Christ, my marriage, my family, my church, my outreach (we were running Alpha in our home), and my work. We were on top of the mountain. I said to Jeannie, "Does life get any better than this?"

> *I have learned that God:*
>
> *- is more concerned about our friendship with Him than in what we do for Him; and*
>
> *- takes us through different seasons and wants us to enjoy Him in each one.*

Season Seven—"You Will Have Trouble, But..."

As good as life had been up to this point, it was about to take a dramatic turn for the worst.

Jesus warned us:

> *In this world you will have trouble.*
> *But take heart! I have overcome the world.*
>
> **John 16:33**

When the terrible darkness came and things started to turn against me, I asked, "Why is this happening to me?" My love for the Lord hadn't changed, and as far as I knew, I hadn't done anything to deserve the intense suffering I was about to experience. So why? I think this is a question that everyone who has experienced suffering has asked.

It's when things don't go according to plan that our faith is tested.

The next few chapters are incredibly painful for me. But please journey with me through the pain. I believe it's in the suffering that hearts are bonded and honest stories are told.

Can we say God loves us only when He answers our prayers and everything is going well, or does He love us even when our prayers are not answered as we want? If the latter, how does God work in and through our suffering? What does the Bible teach about suffering?

Is it possible to experience love, peace, and even joy in the midst of suffering?

As I consider my life and the events that have taken place thus far, I can see the hand of a master craftsman, my loving heavenly Father. Often, in the dark times, I hear a voice in my head telling me it makes no sense and that God has abandoned me. But then, I break out again into the sunlight, and I can see that golden thread of purpose weaving through every circumstance and event, however bad it seemed at the time. This is wonderfully expressed in the following poem.

> *My life is but a weaving*
> *Between my God and me.*
> *I cannot choose the colors*
> *He weaveth steadily.*
> *Oft' times He weaveth sorrow;*
> *And I in foolish pride*
> *Forget He sees the upper*
> *And I the underside.*
> *Not 'til the loom is silent*
> *And the shuttles cease to fly*
> *Will God unroll the canvas*
> *And reveal the reason why.*
> *The dark threads are as needful*
> *In the weaver's skillful hand*
> *As the threads of gold and silver*
> *In the pattern He has planned.*
> *He knows, He loves, He cares;*
> *Nothing this truth can dim.*
> *He gives the very best to those*
> *Who leave the choice to Him.*

42.

The Start of the Darkness

God had clearly led us to purchase our home in Lake Forest. Over coffee, Jeannie reminded me of a conversation she had with Rebecca. Remembering our early years in London, Rebecca said to Jeannie, "It's interesting to me how the Lord has blessed you. Material things have never been a priority for you, and I remember how you told me that Matthew 6:33 was the verse God gave you when you got married. Now look at you." And we laughed.

I loved our life in Lake Forest, but that is where our Valley of Baka (weeping) started. It began after God spoke to me.

God has at times spoken to me very clearly. His voice has never been audible, but in every instance, I knew it was God. I can remember exactly where I was when He spoke to me.

One sunny afternoon in 2004, I was walking into our bathroom, and God said to me, "Gerard, you are going to go through a period of brokenness, but through it, I will glorify My name."

I told Jeannie what God had said to me, but neither of us had any idea how it applied to us.

From that moment, as in the story of Job, it seemed as though Satan had been released to attack our family. Everything started to go wrong.

Work had mostly been good for me, but in my latest role, I had a sense that things were not right. Things got steadily worse until one day, I had a gut-wrenching feeling that I had been betrayed. Promises that had been made to me were not kept. It was such a letdown after the high point of my Year 2000 role.

At the beginning of 2005, Charlie, our chocolate Labrador, had to be put down. If you're a dog lover, you'll understand how painful this was for me. The children had grown up with Charlie, and he had been a big part of our family for more than 13 years. He was a faithful and loving dog, and we had countless wonderful, happy memories of him. After holding him in my arms for the last time, I said goodbye to my Charlie, and I cried as I left the veterinary clinic on that sad day.

A few months later, we were shocked to the core of our being when out of the blue, at a regular eye check, our daughter Rebecca was diagnosed with retinitis pigmentosa (RP). This meant she was slowly going blind. Rebecca was short-sighted, and she had had regular check-ups at Moorfields Hospital, one of the top eye hospitals in the UK. Rebecca wore glasses and contact lenses, and we had been told her eyes were healthy. No one had ever diagnosed her with RP.

RP is an incurable degenerative disease of the retina that is passed down in the genes. That was a mystery, because we had no knowledge of anyone ever having RP on either Jeannie's or my side of the family.

I felt so sad for my daughter and as her dad, I wanted to do everything I could to protect her. Rebecca was so beautiful, brave and courageous, and she never once complained. It broke my heart to think of her losing her sight. We asked our family and friends to pray, and the elders of our church anointed her with oil for healing.

The first answer to prayer was that Rebecca was put under the care of Dr. Fisher, one of the top RP doctors in the country. There are more than two hundred strains of RP. Rebecca's strain of RP progressed very slowly. Although her left eye was quite bad, they said she would be able to live a normal life until well into her 70s. By then, they were hopeful of having a cure.

> *I have learned that it's one thing to trust God is with me when everything is going well, but I had to go to a deeper level of faith and prayer to trust God is still with me when I was hurting and my life had taken a turn for the worst.*

If you have ever had pain and suffering in your life, you will be able to empathize with how I was feeling. How did you get through those difficult days? What happened to your faith and prayer life when you were hurting? Looking back, what would you have done differently?

43.

Nightmare

What is your worst nightmare? Until November 8, 2005, I wouldn't have known how to answer this question. But now I know.

It breaks my heart to tell you about this part of my story. I don't want to go into all the detail. What I will share is some of the pain of that unbelievable night.

Alex, and nothing unusual here, was trying to help a new boy who was struggling in school. Unfortunately, his efforts backfired after they smoked some marijuana together. Alex was not used to the drug and he became strangely paranoid. We talked and prayed together and after hugging and comforting Alex, we strongly believed he was coming through it.

The nightmare started when Jeannie found a suicide note in Alex's bedroom!

What followed was a desperate search for him.

We didn't know where he was. We were in a living hell. We called the police. Between our tears and our prayers, we begged the police to do more. But they told us they were doing all they could. We asked if they could use a helicopter equipped with a thermal-imaging camera but were told it was too windy to fly. We asked about using search and rescue dogs but were told there were no dog handlers available. Everything seemed to be against us; we were surrounded by an atmosphere of confusion.

The police asked us to wait at home in case Alex turned up or contacted us. I couldn't bear to see Jeannie and Rebecca weeping and in such torment. Gathering them in my arms, we cried out to God with all our hearts to save Alex. As the time ticked on, there was little or no relief—we had no news. I pleaded with the Lord for help, and He gave me Psalm 119:165. I didn't recognize the reference; when I looked it up, it meant nothing to me:

> *Great peace have they who love your Word,*
> *and nothing can make them stumble.*

Somewhere in the distance we heard sirens. We looked at each other with tears streaming down our faces. And then, just after midnight, after almost four hours of anguish, waiting, weeping, and praying, there was a knock at our door.

I left Jeannie and Rebecca on the couch, and hoping that this would be the good news we had so desperately been praying for, I hurried to answer the door. As I opened it, I saw a semicircle of people standing there. I immediately recognized Burt, Jim, Sandy, and Scott, some of our friends from church. There were also two police officers, including the officer in charge, whom we had met earlier. After a brief pause, the police officer stepped through the door and held out his hand to me.

"I'm so sorry, Mr. Long. Alex's body has been found at the beach," he said.

Alex had hanged himself.

My strength left me, and I fell to the floor, howling like a wounded animal.

> *I experienced, for the first time in my life, utter and total brokenness.*

44.

Catastrophic Grief

Jeannie and Rebecca had followed me to the front door, and seeing me broken on the floor, started to scream and sob. They fell on the floor with me, and together we wept, if you can call it weeping. It rose from the depths of our stomachs. We could not stop crying.

Time seemed to stand still. I felt as if I was suspended between two worlds. I was between the world that I knew and loved, and a world without Alex.

Through four hours of anguish, I had considered the possibility of Alex taking his life. I had concluded that my happy, fun-loving, handsome, athletic son would never do such a terrible thing. He had so much to live for.

How could such catastrophic horror overtake our family? After all, for the last 25 years, hadn't Jeannie and I surrendered our lives to serve God? We had seen God work miracles in and through our lives. All our children had come to faith in Christ, and we had prayed the blood of Jesus over them from the first day we knew of their conception.

We knew and had stood on the promises in scripture for 25 years. In the four hours of waiting, we had again laid claim to the promises found in scripture. Like this one:

If you say, "The LORD is my refuge," and you make the Most High your dwelling, no harm will overtake you, no disaster will come near your tent. For He will command his angels concerning you to guard you in all your ways; they will lift you up in their hands, so that you will not strike your foot against a stone.

Psalm 91:9-12

Didn't the Bible say, "No harm will overtake you"? No, Alex could not possibly have died. He was only 17 years old. Surely God wouldn't allow this to happen to my son.

But the knock at the door was real, the police officer was real, and his words were real. My son was no longer with us. In one moment, the world I had known and loved with Alex was gone.

We were oblivious to everything else around us. We were finished. Could there be any worse pain? Even to this day I still can't believe what happened and the tears continue.

Suicide of a loved one is considered to be one of the worst traumas a person can suffer. Not only do you grieve the loss of your loved one, but also you have the agony of thinking you could and should have stopped it. A child's suicide is particularly horrific—and this is what happened to us!

How could this be? Why did this happen? Where was God when we so desperately needed Him? Why didn't He answer our cries to rescue Alex? What about His promises to protect His children?

Answers to these and other questions would come in the years of pain and agony that followed that darkest of nights.

I experienced a whole other world of suffering and pain.

45.

Alex's Memorial Service

Before Alex's suicide, we had been planning a special 18th birthday party for him, and now I was planning his funeral service. The line between the living and the dead so troubled my heart. A few days earlier, Alex was with us and so alive, and now they're asking me to choose a coffin for him. Only recently I had been having such fun playing tennis with Alex, and now I'm being asked where we wanted his grave to be. We had been chatting about the English Premier soccer league, and now I'm facing the reality of never seeing him again, this side of heaven.

In my darkest hour, I was helped by the love and prayers of our friends and family. Friends like Bill and Jami and Ed and Dawn flew in from New York to love and support us in our tragedy. My heart was comforted to see them, and I was moved to see the tears rolling down their cheeks as they hugged us.

Alex's suicide almost destroyed Jeannie. She told me she didn't want to come to his memorial service but after praying, she said she would attend with me, Rebecca and Ben. Together, we would honor Alex's life.

The day of Alex's memorial service came. My heart was so crushed, I was on my knees crying out to God to help me in this, the second hardest day of my life. I prayed that my God, whom I loved so much, would help Jeannie, Rebecca, and Ben, and that He would give all of us the grace to get through the day.

The black limousine came to pick us up, but before we even reached the church, Jeannie started to have second thoughts and became distressed. I held her close and whispered, "We are going to get through this together." With Ben on one side, me on the other, and Rebecca close by, we managed to help Jeannie to her seat at the front of the church. But when she saw Alex's casket, Jeannie nearly collapsed, and she let out a piercing scream. Wanting so much to help her, I whispered, "Darling, Alex is not in there, he's in heaven and more alive than we are!"

Tears poured down Jeannie's cheeks. Ben put his arm around his mom, and you could hear them sobbing together. The music and the singing were so moving and, in one song, Jeannie raised her trembling arms in worship. It was a sacrifice of praise and worship.

Rebecca shared memories of her little brother and then read the last few verses in Isaiah 40, ending with

But those who hope in the LORD will renew their strength. They will soar on wings like eagles; they will run and not grow weary, they will walk and not be faint.

In the sanctuary there was a window behind the pulpit, and after the service, several people said they saw an eagle circling while Rebecca and I spoke. That was a comfort to me; I believed it was a sign that God was with us in this overwhelming time of brokenness.

As I gave the eulogy, I looked out through my own tears at Jeannie, Rebecca, Ben, and our family and friends. I had never seen so many people crying at one time. I spoke of my son's loving heart and his wonderful qualities, and yes, I also spoke about the tragedy of his death.

Alex made a terrible mistake. What he did was wrong, but I shared about the comfort and hope we had because Alex had come to faith in Christ. I explained the promise that Jesus had given us in John 11:25-26:

I am the resurrection and the life. The one who believes in me will live, even though they die; and whoever lives by believing in me will never die. Do you believe this?

When Jesus took Alex's place on the cross, He took the punishment for all of his sins, including the sin of suicide. Alex had placed his faith in Jesus and His promises in scripture, and because of this, I could say with absolute confidence that Alex was in heaven enjoying his resurrection life. We would miss Alex everyday, but we knew this was only temporary. We would see him again and be with him through eternity. In our grief, we had a living hope.

The church was packed. Sitting on the front row were Alex's friends from his Loyola Academy athletic team. I could see they were in shock, and wanting to give them hope, I invited them, there and then, to believe in what Jesus had done on the cross for them and to receive Him into their hearts. I asked for those who wanted to put their faith in Christ to stand. There was a pause. A sound like rushing wind—about a hundred of Alex's friends stood up and we prayed for them.

It was a cold gray November day, and a few close family and friends gathered with us at the cemetery. We said our final prayers and words of farewell to our beloved Alex. I put my arm around Jeannie as she wept inconsolably, and I watched as they quietly and gently lowered our son's casket into the grave.

My flesh whispered, "Is this it? Is this the end of Alex? His life was cut so short." But there was another voice within me that said, "No, this is not the end, it's hardly the beginning. Alex is more alive than we are, and we will see him again, and we will spend eternity with him!"

> *I experienced God's grace helping my family and me in our brokenness, and touching the hearts of Alex's friends and others in the midst of tragedy.*

46.

Total Darkness

Our world suddenly came to a standstill. It didn't seem right to me that people were carrying on their everyday lives. Sometimes in a war movie, they capture the moment when a soldier loses his hearing after being close to an explosion. That was us. We were reeling. Dumbfounded. Numb.

Everyone grieves in different ways and at different times. With a physical illness such as the common cold, it's reasonable to expect recovery after a period of time. Grief does not work like that. It impacts the soul, which goes much deeper, is more complex, and should not be measured by time.

What is most important is that everyone should grieve well. A person should be encouraged to allow the grief to freely express itself as naturally as possible. Over the years I've heard several unloving and unhelpful comments on how we should grieve, such as, "Isn't it time she got over what happened?" Or "He just needs to let go and move on." Or "Allow God to heal your broken heart so you can continue with your life."

Well-meaning and often sincerely given, such comments lack the understanding of the impact of grief. Unlike the common cold, grief changes you. It lays your soul bare and impacts you in profound ways. Yes, God will heal your broken heart, but you are never the same person again. Depending on the choices you make in your grief, you become either a better person or a bitter person. You either embrace and welcome your grief, or you suppress it, only for it to haunt you later.

Jeannie, Rebecca, Ben, and I all grieved differently.

Jeannie, her mother's heart in pieces, suffered terribly for several years. After the initial shock of Alex's suicide, she wept and grieved and struggled with her faith. She just couldn't reconcile how a loving God would allow Alex to die in such an evil, cruel, and lonely way.

"If it was his time," she would say, "why didn't God just take him in a more natural way? That would have been hard enough, but not suicide!"

She would quote Scriptures, such as

> *Children are a heritage from the LORD,*
> *offspring a reward from him.*
> **Psalm 127:3**

And she would ask, "Why then has the Lord taken Alex from me?" She would wrestle with the fact that we had served the Lord with all our hearts, and yet He allowed this evil to happen to us.

I tried to comfort Jeannie, but she could not live with the mystery of what had happened. Whatever I said during this season of grief didn't seem to help her. Life and faith in God were no longer making sense to Jeannie. Day after day, I continued to gently speak the truth of God's promises to her, praying that one day she would see again the living hope that God was working through our tragedy as part of His eternal plan and purpose.

What is particularly evil with a suicide is the blame that it can cause. The Bible describes Satan as "the accuser of the brethren" (Revelation 12:10), and he loves to terrorize suicide survivors.

The Lord told me early on, that I was not to even start down the road of blame, and I was acutely aware of Satan trying to attack me in that area. In her grief, Jeannie became locked into a prison of blame and shame.

"Why didn't we do something, anything, to stop Alex's suicide?" she would say. "What terrible parents we must be to have missed the signs."

She would remember decisions that she believed led to his suicide and blamed me for them. "If you hadn't insisted that he went to the large school, Alex would be with us today!"

The questions went around and around in her mind, and the regrets became bigger and bigger. The decisions we could have made leading up to the night of his suicide added more pain to Jeannie.

Then she went back further: "If we had stayed in London or in New York, Alex would still be with us."

I felt helpless as I saw my wife slowly sink into terrible darkness, turning her back on the Lord. I wept for her in prayer as her grief turned to anger and bitterness, and then to hatred. She hated herself, she hated me, and she hated God. The darkness closed around her, as she finally lost her faith in the God who loved her so much.

"How can you believe in a God who would allow such evil to happen to us?" she would ask me. But I knew this wasn't the real Jeannie. I decided that however long it would take, I would fight for her. Satan was not going to have her. But it turned out to be a long and bloody battle.

At night, I would often wake up to Jeannie's inconsolable cries. I had a choice. Should I wake her up from her subconscious nightmare and into her conscious nightmare?

I would gently lay my hand on her and pray for God to comfort her, and I would pray against every evil attack on her and for God's peace to fill her. Usually, she would wake up, and her nightmare would continue, only now she was conscious.

Sometimes, in the middle of the night, Jeannie would run out of the house and up our driveway shouting, "Alex, Alex, Alex, where are you? I'm coming!" Thankfully, I was still quite a fast runner, and the driveway was long enough for me to catch up with Jeannie before she reached the main road. I would hold her in my arms and whisper, "Darling, it's okay, it's okay! Let's go back to the house." She would be delirious in her grief and would be saying over and over again, "No, I need to find Alex, he needs my help, I must find Alex! Alex, Alex!"

"Darling," I would say, "Alex has gone home to heaven ahead of us, and we are going to see him again."

In the early days, our friends called to see how they could help. But after a while, Jeannie asked me, "What are all these people doing in our home?"

"Darling, our friends have called in to see how they can help us."

"Send them away," she said. "I don't want them in my home. Get them out of my home!"

I felt sorry for our friends. They were hurting with us, but I had to protect Jeannie. It was as though she had been terribly burnt, and she couldn't stand having anyone near her.

As the reality set in that Alex wasn't coming back, Jeannie's grief took her into more and more darkness. She pushed away even her closest friends. The last person she pushed away was me.

Ben flew in from the UK as soon as we told him about Alex's death. He stayed a few weeks, allowing us to have some time to grieve together. It was hard when the time came for him to return to the UK and I had to return to work.

It was a pure gift that Rebecca was living at home at this time. In the months and years that followed, she cared for Jeannie and was a wonderful help to me. However, she was so focused on helping Jeannie and in doing her MBA studies at night, I don't think she took the time to properly grieve for her brother. A few years later, she had a partial breakdown, which Jeannie and I believe was related to Alex's suicide.

I have learned that everyone grieves differently, and we must comfort people wherever they are on their journey. Never should we try to speed it up.

47.

How Do You Keep Going?

The question I am most often asked is, "How do you keep going in your suffering?"

I wrote Living Hope in part to answer this universal question.

It would be misleading to simply share a list of actions. The real answer is in the previous 25 years of walking with Christ. Developing spiritual disciplines or habits are helpful when things are going well and they are essential in the storms of life. Storms that will come your way.

When I was in the darkest period of my life, the two years after Alex's suicide, death seemed a better option than life. I never seriously considered suicide, but the thought often crossed my mind. I knew God was my only hope, and I desperately clung to Him.

There were many times when I was at my wit's end. In these times, like the psalmist, I cried out to God, "Oh, Lord, help me. Save me from my adversary who is trying to destroy Jeannie and my family."

Over the years I have always been totally honest with the Lord. My heart was broken and it needed to be healed. I needed to grieve and grieve well and the only one to help me do this was the Holy Spirit. I prayed, "Lord, Jesus said that You are the Comforter, and I ask You to comfort and heal my heart. I surrender all my grief to You. You know me better than I know myself, and I ask that You help me to be open to grieve when I need to. Amen."

God answered my prayer, sometimes at unexpected times. For example, driving to work, a wave of grief would come over me, and tears would flow down my cheeks as I wept from the bottom of my heart.

I learned what the Apostle Paul meant when he wrote of "the fellowship of his sufferings" (Philippians 3:10).

There were also times, in the early days after Alex's death, when I wrestled with God. I asked, "Why?"

"Oh, God, why did You allow this to happen? Lord, we served You with all our hearts for all these years! I thought I had surrendered everything to You!"

By the way, it's okay to throw your pain and anger, and your questions at God. It's been going on for thousands of years, and He's big enough to handle it. In fact, the Bible encourages us to do so. It tells us to "Cast all your cares on to Him because He cares for you" (1 Peter 5:7).

In those dark and painful times, God drew near to me by His Holy Spirit. I felt His love in my grieving heart, and He comforted me.

Scripture has always been at the core of my walk with Christ and God's promises sustained me through the storm. I memorized God's word and I meditated upon it day and night. There is spiritual power released in God's word and I highly recommend it as the source of true meditation.

As God drew near to me, I praised and worshiped Him in the midst of the storm.

It's a paradox that alongside the sweet times I had with God, I was also engaged in a mighty fight of faith. Satan's goal was to destroy my trust in God and I had to remain strong and vigilant to engage in the fierce spiritual battle.

In my times with God, He gave me three epiphanies that comforted my heart, gave me great hope, and strengthened me for the battle ahead for Jeannie, Rebecca, and Ben. And He laid the foundation stones for my purpose, a courageous warrior spirit to help others.

The Bible talks about finding treasure in the darkness (Isaiah 45:3), and this is what I discovered.

48.

The First Epiphany - The Throne of Grace

The first treasure, the first epiphany that God gave me in the darkness, was a deeper understanding of His grace. Grace is God's provision for us through Jesus Christ—the salvation of our souls through Jesus' sacrifice on the cross for eternity and for everyday living. In giving us His victorious life, we can receive the comfort, love, courage, strength, wisdom, finances, everything we need each day, to do His will (Hebrews 13:20-21)—including, for me, strength to journey through brokenness and to fight for my family. I held to God's promise that, "My grace is sufficient for you" (2 Corinthians 12:9).

Taking the encouragement from the following Scripture, I became a regular visitor at the throne of grace:

> *Let us then approach God's throne of grace with confidence,*
> *so that we may receive mercy and find grace*
> *to help us in our time of need.*
> ### Hebrews 4:16

I would often spend several hours a night crying out to God. I was desperate for His mercy and grace in my time of great need.

Alex's suicide broke our hearts. I knew nothing would be the same again. But I didn't expect it to wreck our marriage. My heart grieved for Alex and my marriage, and I knew that God's love was my only hope. I was fighting for Jeannie as I cried out to God, and He poured His love into my heart. Each day I would wake up and experience God's love giving me strength and fresh hope.

Jeannie refused my love day after day, and I ended each day exhausted and drained. I remember two occasions when I was particularly discouraged and said to God, "This is too much for me. I can't go on. But if You want me to continue, I need more of Your love and grace."

The miracle is that when I got up the next morning, I again found I had fresh love in my heart.

> *I have learned that:*
>
> *- God's grace is sufficient for me, and whatever He may ask me to do for Him, He will provide everything I need to complete the task;*
>
> *- I must go boldly to God's Throne of Grace, to receive what I need for each new day; and*
>
> *- God's glory is revealed in the grace He provides to journey on in the midst of the storm.*

49.

The Second Epiphany - The Eternal Perspective

I received the second epiphany in the stillness, between the tears, as God's love soothed my wounded heart. He gave me a deep understanding of eternity. The Bible says, "He has planted eternity in the human heart" (Ecclesiastes 3:11), and in my brokenness, I could see what it is.

This gave me comfort and great hope. This life is fleeting! It's the preparation for the eternal life to come.

Seeing eternity changes everything. I saw and understood the Scriptures highlighting that this life is like a vapor, a breath (James 4:14, Job 14:1-2, Psalm 39:5, 1 Peter 1:24), relative to what is to come. Because Alex had received Christ, I believed what the Bible said about his eternal state. He isn't dead but is more alive than we are. We are going to see him again. C.S. Lewis said, "This life is the cover page of a never-ending story."

I received a revelation of God's heart for His lost children—lost for eternity. I understood His plan of salvation on another level. I saw that the age we live in now is the time of decision—decision to receive or reject God's saving grace in Jesus Christ. It's decision time for those who have received Him to surrender their lives for His eternal plan and purpose. Every day, God is giving each person another chance, another day to be rescued for eternity.

I desperately miss Alex every day. But, I believe with all my heart that I will see him again. I also believe that anything God asks me to go through in this life will be rewarded one hundredfold now and through eternity (Mark 10:28-31, Luke 18:29-30). The following Scripture summarizes what I discovered.

For our light and momentary troubles are achieving for us an eternal glory that far outweighs them all. So we fix our eyes not on what is seen, but on what is unseen, since what is seen is temporary, but what is unseen is eternal.

2 Corinthians 4:17-18

I have learned that seeing eternity changes how I view everything, and it sets me free from the things of this world, to fully serve God.

50.

The Third Epiphany - God's Heart for the Suffering

The third epiphany God showed me in my dark nights of the soul was His love and the depth of His heart for the suffering. Often in our grief, we forget that God knows our pain and is grieving with us.

I remember it so clearly. In a time of intense weeping, I felt an arm around my shoulder. It was so real that I looked up. I knew in that moment that Jesus was there with me. In these sacred moments, He seemed closer than my breath, and He was weeping with me. Right there and then, I realized how God's heart breaks for all the suffering in the world. He sees it all and He loves every person.

If you're suffering, I want you to know that God sees you and He loves you. He wants to hold you and comfort you in your pain.

One may struggle with the question, "Why doesn't God stop all the suffering?" It's a good and an appropriate question.

The day will come when God stops all the suffering. When Jesus returns, He will restore this world to the way God originally intended it to be. We are heading for a time and place with God where there will be no more death or mourning or crying or pain (Revelation 21:4).

But when that day does come, and it will come, the time for decision will be over.

In this age, God's love has given us free will—to accept Him or reject Him. However, at the beginning of creation, God warned us that the consequence of rejecting Him and going our own way would be death and disorder. This is what we see today across the world pain, suffering and evil. It's all around us. God respects our decision to reject Him, not just for now but also through eternity.

I saw that God wanted to redeem Jeannie and me from our pain and suffering. I took hold of His promise to restore us and empower us to triumph over the evil that had devastated our family. Our sovereign God would turn the evil around for good, giving us the grace and courage to give comfort and hope to others.

As I looked through the Bible, I saw that God first tried and tested in the furnace of suffering the people that He used—Joseph, Job, David, Paul, and of course, Jesus Himself. It was through the dying to self that His life came forth. The power of the cross of Christ—the most gruesome and yet the most loving event in human history! Through the cross, God provided a rescue plan for the world.

As Jesus said, "Very truly I tell you, unless a kernel of wheat falls to the ground and dies, it remains only a single seed. But if it dies, it produces many seeds." (John 12:24). Similarly, God's life flows through our broken vessels.

> *I have learned:*
>
> *- Of God's heart for the suffering and for His mercy on humankind, giving us more time, because He doesn't want anyone to perish;*
>
> *- That the power of the cross flows through our broken vessels; and*
>
> *- That in God's kingdom, our suffering is never meaningless—God always wants to turn it for good.*

51.

Epiphanies

An epiphany is a great revelation that changes you in some way.

My epiphanies were a gift from God, and they gave me much-needed hope in my pain and suffering. Over the last 16 years, they have helped to encourage and inspire me, to shepherd and guide me to God's calling on my life. My purpose!

In my darkest times, when my pain was so great, I felt as if I couldn't go on. I questioned what God was doing. I discovered an anchor for my soul. It is that God loves me. Whatever He may have permitted in my life is part of His eternal plan and purpose, and He will use it for His glory and my eternal blessing. My challenge is to trust Him in my pain. The following Scripture has helped me to keep going:

Trust in the LORD with all your heart and lean not on your own understanding; in all your ways submit to him, and he will make your paths straight.

Proverbs 3:5-6

I have learned that all I ever see is a small amount of what is actually going on, and I am totally dependent on the Lord to guide and equip me on my journey through life.

52.

Grief upon Grief

Only two months after Alex passed, I received a phone call from my brother Will. He sounded so sad.

"Hi, G," he said, calling me by the nickname my family used since I was a child. "I'm sorry to have to tell you this, but I have some bad news."

I braced myself. He continued. "It's Jax. She's just had another round of chemo, and it's affected her very badly. G, I'm sorry but she is not expected to live for more than a few hours."

A wave of emotion surged from within me. I loved Jax, and she loved me. As the firstborn and my only sister, she made me feel so special. And it was Jax that had led me to the Lord when I was only five years old.

Jax was beautiful and gregarious. But she had had two painful marriages. On top of this, she was treated for breast cancer several years before. After treatment, she was given the all-clear, and we thanked God that she was cancer-free.

A few years later, she started having agonizing back pain. For 11 months, she went back and forth to the medical professionals, and they kept misdiagnosing her. I was surprised and devastated when Jax was finally diagnosed with advanced bone cancer.

They started Jax on chemotherapy, but the cancer was so advanced that she had to have a bone graft to prevent her tibia from snapping.

As Will and I continued our conversation, my tears started to well up from within.

"I'm so sorry, Will. I thought she was going to recover. This has happened so fast. I'm going to catch the first plane I can—please ask her to hang on until I get there."

"I'll tell her you're coming and that you want her to hold on, but I'm not sure she'll make it," Will replied.

"I understand," I said.

"G, I'm sorry to have to give you this news on top of what you are going through."

Will had compassion for what I was going through and I looked forward to his weekly phone calls.

"Thanks, Will," I managed to say between sobs. "I'll see you soon."

I slumped to the floor and started to weep uncontrollably.

I managed to get an overnight flight to London Heathrow, praying that the Lord would miraculously heal my sister.

I drove to the hospice where my mother, my brothers Kim and Will, Jax's husband Brian, her daughters Jo and Fiona, and other close family and friends were waiting. Will had passed my message on to Jax, and she had made it through the night.

They warned me that the chemo had changed her, but I was shocked by what I saw. There on the bed was a shriveled-up version of my beautiful sister. I hardly recognized her. She was barely alive, unconscious and gasping for every breath.

Someone told me that the last sense to go is hearing, so I sat up close and spoke a few words into her ear.

"Jax, it's G, I got here as soon as I could." I didn't notice any response, but I was trusting she could hear me. I wanted her to know I was there.

"I love you, Jax," I continued, as she struggled for every breath. "Thank you for being such a loving sister to me. I will never forget that it was you that led me to receive Jesus as my Savior."

"You're going to see Jesus soon," I said, "and I want you to do something for me. Please, will you give Alex a hug from me and Jeannie?"

It was a sacred moment. The tears were flowing.

I had to use the bathroom, and while I was out of the room Jax was promoted to heaven. I believe her love for me and God's grace had enabled her to hold on until I arrived. Within the next hour, she had passed.

My mom told me that just before Jax passed, she suddenly sat up and opened her eyes as if she was looking at someone. She then slumped back on the bed, and she was gone. We believe that Jax's body was manifesting what her spirit was seeing in heaven. It was wonderful to think that she was seeing Jesus.

This was a confirmation of what the Lord had been showing me about eternity. This life is a vapor. It's a preparation for what is to come, and for those who are in Jesus Christ, when our body on earth dies, God has prepared for us a body in heaven that will last forever.

For we know that if the earthly tent we live in is destroyed, we have a building from God, an eternal house in heaven, not built by human hands.

2 Corinthians 5:1

We are confident, yes, well pleased rather to be absent from the body and to be present with the Lord.

2 Corinthians 5:8

I discovered that when you are in the midst of a nightmare, you can still get more bad news.

53.

Amazing Grace

It was hard to leave my family in England so soon after Jax's funeral, but I needed to get back to Jeannie.

After a long trip back to my home in Lake Forest, in the midst of grief upon grief, I was emotionally, mentally, and physically exhausted. I had missed Jeannie and had been praying that the Lord would comfort her. I was hoping she would be pleased to see me.

"Hi darling, I've missed you," I said, as I went to hug and kiss her. But she turned away from my embrace.

"This is a nightmare," she said, glaring at me. "Tell me, why did you bring us to the U.S. in the first place? We were so happy in the UK, and our family was all together. If you hadn't brought us here, Alex would still be alive!"

"Darling, do we have to go over this again?" I asked.

"Yes, we do," Jeannie snapped back at me. "I just can't understand why you didn't listen to me."

"You never listen to me!" Jeannie shouted. "I didn't want to come here, and you didn't listen to me when I wanted to go after Alex that night."

I tried to reason with Jeannie. "Darling, of course, we would have done things differently if we knew what was going to happen, but we didn't know, and it doesn't help blaming me and trying to wind back the clock. Both our hearts are broken, and I want us to grieve together," I said.

"Why would I want to grieve with you?" Jeannie snarled. "I hate you, and I hate what you have done."

It felt as though Satan himself was trying to finish me off!

I don't know how I survived those dark and terrible days. All I can say is that it was a miracle of God's amazing grace.

During this time, I clung to this Scripture:

> *God is my refuge, He is the one who sustains me.*
> **Psalm 54:4**

It's a testament to God's faithfulness that He always sustained me.

> *I have learned that Satan can directly attack us through the people we love.*

54.

Comfort and Help

Jeannie was inconsolable in the weeks, months, and years after Alex's suicide.

I prayed about getting help. Our church recommended a Christian psychiatrist. In the first session with him, we showed him Alex's suicide note.

"In all my 30 years of psychiatry, I have never seen a note like this. It's so spiritual," he said. His comment confirmed to us how confused and paranoid Alex had become after smoking marijuana. In the two additional sessions we had with him, he didn't connect with us, and his advice wasn't based on scripture.

Although he didn't work out, Jeannie did get help from some close friends and a counselor from our church who visited her every day and walked with her through her grief and pain.

After a couple of years, one of her close friends suggested it might be healthy if she found a part-time job linked to her love for children. Jeannie was a teacher, and her friend directed her to a couple of part-time teaching positions. She got a job taking care of two young boys.

Jeannie's work with the boys was such an answer to prayer, helping her through the next phase of her grief. Her counselor encouraged her and walked her through this season, telling her to lay her grief at the front door of the boys' house and pick it up again when she went home. Jeannie became very fond of the boys and they of her, and it was a sad day when the job ended.

> *I have learned that comfort and help for the suffering can come in different ways, and it's important to be open to how the Holy Spirit is directing you to help others or receive help.*

55.

Modern-Day Saint

Rebecca wrote in her journal, "I would never have imagined that my heart would be broken by my little brother!"

Rebecca was a beautiful and talented young woman. When I say she was beautiful, I'm not just saying it as her father. Others said how lovely she was.

Rebecca had long, dark hair, sparkling green eyes, and her smile lit up a room. She had an athletic physique, and as you can imagine, she had many admirers. But, she was trusting the Lord to lead her to marry a man who loved Jesus as she did.

Some people described Rebecca as a modern-day saint. Her lovingkindness touched many people's hearts.

For a young person, Rebecca walked at such a depth with Jesus. She had some heartbreaking challenges but she never got bitter or angry with God. Instead, she looked for ways to help other people who were suffering.

In her grief-induced depression, Jeannie would stay in her bed, too weak to get up. At first, Rebecca stayed by her side. Several months later, Rebecca, knowing that it wasn't healthy for her to stay in a dark room, encouraged Jeannie to get up and go for coffee.

"Please get up, Mom, have your shower, and let's go for a cup of coffee," Rebecca would say.

Jeannie would answer, "No, I'm not getting up. Go away."

While Jeannie refused my help, over time she did accept Rebecca's love and help. I think that deep inside, she was touched by her courage.

After talking back and forth several times, Rebecca would pull the covers off Jeannie, help her to get ready, and then go for a drive-through coffee.

Among the few moments of happiness I had in those days were the evening talks I had with Rebecca, discussing how her day had gone and how Jeannie had been with her. Rebecca was gentle and kind, and so brave in helping her mom while her own heart was broken for Alex. I know it hurt her to see how Jeannie was treating me and how our once beautiful marriage was hanging by a thread.

As the weeks rolled into months, Rebecca and I became more and more concerned for Jeannie. She often said, "I wish I had never been born!"—the same words Job spoke in Job 3:1. Increasingly, she was saying, "I am going to take my life!"

The tipping point was a phone call I received from one of Jeannie's close friends.

"Hi, Gerard," her friend said. "I'm calling because I'm concerned about Jeannie." She continued, "More and more, she's talking about taking her life. For her own safety, have you considered admitting her to a psychiatric hospital?"

"Yes," I answered. "You have confirmed what Rebecca and I were thinking."

But taking Jeannie to a psychiatric hospital proved to be a horrible experience.

I have learned, at another level, how brave my daughter is.

56.

Psychiatric Hospital

It was a cold, gray day when Rebecca and I took Jeannie to be admitted to the local psychiatric hospital. We thought it would be best if Jeannie was cared for by some professionals, in a warm and loving environment. We were in for a shock.

As we went through the door and approached the reception desk, we thought it could have been a normal hospital. But, as soon as we started talking to the receptionist, I realized this was different. The young lady showed little or no emotion or concern about Jeannie's condition. Instead, she made it clear that once Jeannie was registered and we went through the doors at the end of the corridor, she would not be allowed out unless a registered doctor signed her out.

Rebecca and I glanced at each other, and I knew we were thinking the same thing. Knowing Jeannie, I had grave concerns she wouldn't do well in a locked environment, but if we took her home, there was a risk she could take her life.

In the moment, we decided it was right to proceed, and Rebecca and I escorted Jeannie through doors that slammed and locked behind us. This began an experience I never want to go through again. I won't go into all the details, but suffice it to say that the attitude of all but one of the people who dealt with us on that day was that

Jeannie was a dangerous person. To us, it seemed as though they were treating Jeannie as if they were afraid she might lash out at someone at any moment. It was demeaning and frightening.

To our horror, she was escorted away by an officious nurse and a huge, menacing guard. Jeannie was told to take everything off and put on a white gown. Rebecca and I were handed her belongings in a plastic bag. To this point, Rebecca had been unbelievably strong, but seeing Jeannie's belongings in a plastic bag—her mother was nowhere to be seen—she let out a mighty scream: "Please, let my mom out!"

We were told that Jeannie would be in a ward with 20 other patients with a wide range of mental health issues. She would be given medication to minimize the risk of her taking her own life.

Jeannie was already being watched by two armed guards, and there was little opportunity for us to talk together. Through whispers and nonverbal communication, Rebecca and I decided that leaving her there was a terrible idea. Jeannie hated taking drugs and we knew she would be terrified if she ended up in a ward with the other patients. She might totally lose her mind!

I spoke to one of the doctors and told her we had decided this was not the right course of action for Jeannie. We wanted to take her home. Things now got scary. The doctor told me we no longer had any rights to remove Jeannie. She would be assessed by a doctor, and if Jeannie was deemed to be a threat to herself or others, she would be admitted to the ward.

Jeannie's long-term sanity depended on how the doctor assessed her. Considering the things she was saying and how she was acting, it didn't look good.

Rebecca and I found a quiet room and prayed for God's help. We contacted our close friends to ask them to cry out to God for Jeannie. It was critical that Jeannie somehow came to her senses for the assessment with the doctor.

The first answer to prayer was that they allowed me back in to see Jeannie. While I was with her, she wanted to go to the bathroom, which was another answer to prayer—she wasn't allowed to be on her own, so they let me go with her. While we were in the bathroom, I whispered in Jeannie's ear, "Just be yourself."

Jeannie looked at me, laughed, and said, "They will definitely keep me in if I do that."

In this bit of humor, which I hadn't seen for many months, I had some hope. I believed our prayers were being answered.

The assessing doctor was a large, scary man. He had the same attitude we had experienced all morning—Jeannie was guilty unless she could prove her innocence. It was touch and go, but the prayers were working, because he decided to have Jeannie assessed by another doctor.

The next doctor who saw Jeannie had some common sense and compassion. It was another answer to our prayers. When she heard our story, she realized that immobilizing Jeannie with drugs and admitting her to a mental health ward was not what she needed.

With thankful hearts, Rebecca and I were delighted to gather Jeannie up in our arms and take her home.

> *I experienced again that God is near at hand to rescue us in our time of need!*

57.

"I Do Want to Live!"

A few weeks later, I awoke, and Jeannie was not in our bed. Alarmed, I got up and began to look through the house for her. Rebecca heard me calling, and she joined me in looking for Jeannie. We found her downstairs, groaning on the floor in the living room. She was in anguish from a terrible pain in her stomach and was almost passing out from the agony. We called 911. Thankfully, an ambulance arrived in only a few minutes and rushed her to the hospital.

A grueling day of tests revealed that her intestines had doubleknotted, and if left untreated, she would die. Two of our new friends at church were Mark and Susan. As it turned out, Mark was the chief executive officer of the hospital Jeannie had been taken to. He was generous to us and arranged for the best surgeon on staff to do an emergency operation on Jeannie.

As Jeannie was waiting to go into the operating room, I was allowed to see her. As I looked into her eyes, it suddenly struck me that this might be the last time that I would see my precious Jeannie. Seeing my grief and pain, Jeannie called me over, and in a weak, whispery voice she said, "Gerard, I do want to live!"

In answer to my prayers and the prayers of our friends, as Jeannie said that, my heart filled with more hope that her broken heart was healing.

I thanked God that her operation was successful. I was grateful to have help from Rebecca and some friends, and over the next twelve months or so, Jeannie convalesced and made a full recovery.

> *I experienced God's grace coming to us through the kindness of Mark and Susan, Page, Angelika, and other friends who helped save Jeannie's life and care for her until she recovered.*

58.

Church

In the early days after Alex's suicide, I was still numb but would go to church on my own. While I was at church, Jeannie would do her usual morning routine of walking to the tree where Alex took his life and then to his grave. Sometimes she would lay on his grave, sobbing.

On one cold, snowy Sunday morning, the Lord spoke to me while I was in church.

He said, "Gerard, you need to be with Jeannie."

The service had just started. I stood up, walked out, and went to look for Jeannie. I found her halfway between the tree and Alex's grave. I could see she was freezing, and her tears had left a mark down her cheeks.

At this stage, Jeannie still hated me and didn't want anything to do with me. I wasn't sure how she would react in seeing me. I didn't want to say anything that would turn her away from me. All I ended up doing was holding out my hand to Jeannie through the car window. Thankfully, to my surprise and delight, she got into the car. We didn't speak, but I was so glad to have Jeannie beside me and out of the cold.

From that time on, I would be with Jeannie every Sunday morning. I would go out and buy us a coffee, and we would sit quietly, sipping our drinks and sharing a chocolate chip cookie. I was just happy to be with her. And I knew it was where God wanted me to be.

It was important for me to have some spiritual fellowship. God provided times of prayer and sharing with guys at church and at work. Best of all, Mark, my long-term friend and prayer partner, would come around to my house early one morning each week. Mark is another Brit, and our conversation flowed easily from my grief to Jeannie's progress, the Scriptures God was impressing on our hearts, and even to our mutual love of rugby. It was a bit of light relief, although I had to make an allowance, because Mark is a keen Welsh supporter, and Wales is an archrival of England in the Six Nations Championship! We ended our time together in prayer and worship.

Every step of Jeannie's healing was hard and I covered it in prayer. I wanted her to start meeting with other Christians and, one Sunday morning, I asked her to join me in meeting with George and Judy, and to my surprise, she agreed. Jeannie has since told me that although she felt nothing inside, she knew it was the right thing to do.

George loves the Lord Jesus. He has a big heart, he loves people, is a natural leader, has a great sense of humor, and is a gifted musician. George is the life and soul of the party and one of my closest friends.

Judy has the warmest, smiling face you can imagine, which reflects her love for Jesus Christ and other people. She has lots of stories about growing up in Kenya as a missionary's kid and a wonderful heart to help people. She is a gifted worship leader and loves to bless people in her home with her warm and generous hospitality.

George and Judy embraced and loved us as though we were their own family. We felt so close to them, and because they are anglophiles, they loved hearing about when we lived in England.

We met at George and Judy's house, and took turns buying Starbucks coffee. They went out of their way to comfort Jeannie and even gave her a chair that they said was hers. For a long time, Jeannie would sit quietly in her chair listening as the three of us chatted, encouraged each other in God's Word, and worshiped God.

The presence of the Lord filled the room, and although we were together for two to three hours each time, it would seem like only a few minutes! I've learned that God's presence brings freedom, allowing us to be our real selves. Over time, Jeannie started to share her thoughts in our time together.

One beautiful sunny Sunday morning, Jeannie and I were walking up George and Judy's driveway, when we heard some heavenly music. George welcomed us, and there was Judy playing the piano. It was a tune the Lord had given her to play, albeit, in a key she had never played in before. Judy told us that the Lord gave her the tune in memory of Alex. We sat in awe and wonder. Jeannie wept.

My heart was filled with joy as I watched Jeannie heal during our Sunday mornings together.

After two or three years, we felt the Lord wanted us to invite others to enjoy the fellowship. On Friday evenings, George and Judy opened their home for the meetings, and that was the start of our house church. The evening started and ended with a lot of talk and laughter around a table full of delicious food that Judy prepared. George was brilliant at welcoming people and would open with a prayer, Judy would lead an anointed praise and worship time, and I would teach from the Bible. I was thankful that Rebecca encouraged Jeannie to join these meetings.

They would sit together at the back of the room so Jeannie could leave if she needed to.

> *I experienced how God can bring beauty from ashes and how wonderful it is when Christians meet together in love, fellowship and harmony. To give hope, living hope, in the midst of tragedy.*

59.

Alpha USA

God's love in my heart has given me a deep concern for the lost. The compelling vision of heaven and eternity I received in my midnight prayer times gave me an urgency to help rescue souls for Christ.

About six months after Alex passed, my friend and prayer partner Mark arranged for me to have a breakfast meeting with David, the chairman of Alpha USA. I immediately liked David, and we became friends with him and his wife Tina. Jeannie and I had to go to London around this time as part of the process of getting our Green Cards (Permanent Resident Cards). While we were there, we had a cup of tea with Nicky and Pippa. Nicky is the pioneer of the Alpha course and was then the curate at Holy Trinity Brompton Church.

When I returned to the America, David asked me to help lead Alpha USA. Alpha was already close to my heart and I had led more than fifty courses since 1995, in our home, the workplace, prison, church, and other locations. I loved the thought of giving all my time to help rescue souls for eternity.

To accept the offer, I would have to give up my 30 year banking career as well as the safe and secure future opportunities HSBC offered me. After prayer and confirmation from some close friends and family, I had to discuss the offer with Jeannie. Reluctantly, Jeannie agreed to sit down with me, and over a coffee and a chocolate chip cookie, I shared my heart for what I believed God was calling me to do. Jeannie had been proud of my career with the bank, and she burst into tears at the thought of me giving it all up.

I was surprised when she said, "If this is what you want to do, who am I to stand in your way?"

So I stepped down from my senior management role with HSBC and took up a new role with Alpha USA.

I knew there would be some challenges ahead. Ben had even said, "Dad, how could you give up your banking career?" However, I had peace in my heart, trusting that God would guide me and work out the details.

The Alpha role meant taking a 70 percent drop in salary. God went before us so that we didn't have to sell our house. We were grieving for Alex, and the last thing I wanted was a house move.

God's ways are so much higher than our ways—He enabled us to stay in our home. There was no way my reduced salary would cover our mortgage payments, but I qualified for a special interest rate with another bank, and we didn't have to move. Just after I received the mortgage funds, the bank stopped the new product. It was almost as if they had started the product just to meet my need!

I was proud to lead Alpha USA. I loved the mission, the work, and the people. The goal was to help spread the good news of Jesus Christ across America, in the most efficient and effective way possible, using the Alpha course.

Thousands of churches were running Alpha. In my last two or three years working for Alpha USA, we estimated that annually, up to a 250,000 people made a first commitment or re-commitment to Christ.

Along with all the fruit came some painful challenges.

One of the challenges we constantly faced was financial. As a non-profit organization, most of our funding came from individuals, churches, and foundations, and most of this was unscheduled. We didn't know when the funds would come in.

We had to live by faith, especially when the biweekly payroll had to be paid. Of course, I remembered when Jeannie and I had to trust God month to month in the first two years of our marriage. But this was much harder, because this time approximately seventy individuals and families were expecting their next paycheck.

I would have a cash-flow meeting with our finance manager at the beginning of each week, and at most of the meetings, we wouldn't know where the funds were coming from to meet that Friday's payroll. The pressure was relentless. I would get up early most mornings to cry out to God for help.

It's in challenges that our faith has the opportunity to grow, and I discovered another level of God's grace. I experienced more of the victorious life of Jesus that is revealed to us by the Holy Spirit.

He will glorify me, because it is from me that he will receive what he will make known to you.
John 16:14

In the midst of the pressure, I had joy and peace. In my eight years at Alpha USA, we never once missed a payroll. Again and again, we witnessed gifts coming through at the eleventh hour, and we thanked and praised God for His provision.

As the Holy Spirit transforms us into the image of Jesus—a process known as sanctification—there is a mighty struggle that takes place with our flesh, the devil, and the world (2 Corinthians 3:18 and Romans 12:2). The Greek word used in the Bible for transformation is metamorphosis, the process by which a caterpillar turns into a butterfly. Think of the struggle the butterfly has as it emerges from its chrysalis. And yet in the struggle, it is being strengthened and prepared for its new life.

I try not to complain to God when I feel the pressure, but I often have to ask for forgiveness for slipping up! One night when I was telling the Lord how weak I felt, He reminded me of a conversation He had with the Apostle Paul:

Three different times I begged the Lord to take it away. Each time he said, "My grace is all you need. My power works best in weakness." So now I am glad to boast about my weaknesses, so that the power of Christ can work through me. That's why I take pleasure in my weaknesses, and in the insults, hardships, persecutions, and troubles that I suffer for Christ. For when I am weak, then I am strong.

2 Corinthians 12:8-10

It was the last few words that got to me. No one wants to feel weak, and yet in God's kingdom, we are at our strongest when we are weak and totally dependent on the Lord! I drove home with a smile on my face as I realized I was in the sweet spot of God's calling and purpose for my life.

It's not so much what we're going through but how we're going through life!

I have learned that when God is working in me in the furnace of trouble and affliction, I must rely on His grace and wait for Him to change things. I must not relieve the pressure through my own actions, but I need to wait for God's perfect timing (Psalm 27:14).

Biblical examples of failing to wait on God's timing include Abraham siring Ishmael (and subsequently, Islam) when he didn't wait for the promise of a son through Sarai, and Saul, who lost his kingdom when he didn't wait for Samuel.

60.

Alpha USA's Newest Employee

Rebecca completed her MBA and had the opportunity to have a glittering career in the corporate world.

Rebecca was shocked by Alex's suicide, and she couldn't stand the thought of a young person dying without giving their heart to Jesus Christ. She wanted to win as many young people to Christ as possible. She was also sensitive to other people's pain in their grief, and whenever she heard about a suicide, she would write a letter of comfort and hope to the siblings of the deceased.

She turned away from pursuing her own career. Sensing the call of God on her life to work with young people, to my great delight, she decided to join me in working with Alpha USA. She became the national director of Alpha Youth.

I loved driving to work with Rebecca every morning. At a certain point on our ride, we would pray together for the day ahead and for her friends to come to know the Lord. On Fridays we would treat ourselves by buying a Starbucks coffee on the way to work.

The Alpha USA staff loved Rebecca. As she grew in her role, I shared speaking engagements with her throughout the country.

61.

The Gift of Dogs

Rebecca said to me one morning, "Hey Dad, you know how much mom loves dogs? Ever since Charlie died, she has wanted another one."

"Yes," I replied, guessing where this was going.

"Well," said Rebecca. "How about getting mom a surprise puppy?"

"That's a great idea," I said. I was eager for anything that might help Jeannie in her grief, and I loved the thought of having another dog. "What sort of dog are you thinking of?"

"I've done some research, and golden retrievers are said to be gentle and loving," she answered.

"Sounds good," I said, "and my friend loves goldens, and he currently has three. I'll ask him for the name of a good breeder." Jeannie and I had gone to dinner at the home of my friend and his wife a few years before, and we had met his three goldens. After we were seated, he let them in the room—and they went berserk at meeting us. They were all over us, and we loved them. My friend called them the terrorists.

My friend was only too pleased to recommend his breeder to us. Rebecca followed up with her boyfriend, Brock, who also had a golden. Later, she visited the breeder, and in deciding everything was good, she put in our order for a golden retriever puppy.

When the time came, Rebecca and I sneaked off to pick up the new puppy, leaving Jeannie at home. We had filled the car with blankets, newspapers, and paper towels, and we were so excited as we set off.

When we arrived at the breeder, the owner welcomed us and sat us down to go over some final items. While we were talking, we could hear some bangs and scratching and quite a commotion coming from the next room.

"What's all that noise?" I asked the owner.

"Oh," said the owner, "that one's yours. She's quite a madam. I was going to keep her as a show dog, but I decided to let you have her."

With that, the breeder opened the door, and in came a bundle of golden fur. From the start, we knew she was a special dog, and so it turned out to be.

When we arrived home, I went in first, leaving Rebecca and the puppy outside. I asked Jeannie to close her eyes and hold out her arms.

Rebecca came in with the bundle of life and fur, and placed the puppy in Jeannie's arms.

"Ahhh!" Jeannie screamed, as she opened her eyes to her new puppy.

I told Jeannie that this was all Rebecca's idea. While still holding the puppy tightly near her face and with tears in her eyes, she thanked and hugged Rebecca.

"What do you want to call her?" I asked Jeannie.

"I want Rebecca to decide," she answered.

"Well, Dad helped in getting the puppy," Rebecca said. "Let's name her after his football team."

And so, Jeannie's new puppy was named Chelsea. I was so happy to see Jeannie love her new dog. From the start, they were inseparable. Whenever Jeannie was grieving Alex, Chelsea would come and sit beside her and comfort her as she wept. They had a special bond. When we went for walks and the ground became uneven or difficult, Chelsea would come back to make sure Jeannie was okay.

As well as being gentle and loving, Chelsea had a special personality and was very intelligent.

Chelsea loved to play. Her favorite game was chase. When I arrived home from work, she would keep dropping a tennis ball on me to throw for her, and she would nudge my leg to get up and chase her. We decided the only way to keep her occupied was to get another golden.

That's how we ended up with Chloe. She certainly kept Chelsea busy.

Chelsea and Chloe gave us years of love, joy, and laughter. As with countless parts of God's creation, a dog gives us a great example of unconditional love. Even if you're only out of the room for a few minutes, the dog is so excited to see you again. Dogs are loyal and faithful, and all they want to do is please you.

I have learned how God can use a dog to help bring comfort and healing to a broken heart.

62.

Glimmers of Love and Light

Over the years, God touched Jeannie in various ways, and each time, a glimmer of His love broke into her darkness.

One cold morning, Rebecca managed to persuade Jeannie to go to Starbucks with her. Venturing out was a bit risky, because Jeannie didn't want to be seen. She would cover up with sunglasses, a hat, and a scarf. On this particular morning, the love of the Lord came through a friend.

As Rebecca and Jeannie stood in line for their coffees, our friend George spotted Jeannie and tapped her on the shoulder.

"Is that you, Jeannie?" George asked.

Not expecting this, Jeannie nodded.

With his heart full of compassion for Jeannie's grief, he asked, "Can I give you a hug?"

With that, George hugged Jeannie and went on his way. He didn't say anything else. He didn't need to. The hug said it all.

Jeannie and Rebecca told me later that day about George's God-filled hug. It was a glimmer of God's loving kindness that reached Jeannie in her grief and vulnerability.

Grief comes in waves, and one time when Jeannie was having a particularly bad day, God's love touched her through creation. It was a snowy, cold winter day, which reflected Jeannie's mood. She came downstairs to make a cup of tea. Gazing out of the window, she thought she saw a piece of red ribbon caught in one of the trees.

With the white background, the red ribbon stood out. Pulling on her coat and boots, Jeannie ventured out into the snowy garden to find out what it was.

As she walked toward the red ribbon, Jeannie realized it wasn't a ribbon at all. It was a red cardinal. The curious thing was, the cardinal seemed as interested in Jeannie as she was in it, and it couldn't seem to take its eyes off her.

The cold soon got to Jeannie, and she went back inside, but every time she looked outside, the cardinal seemed to be watching her. Later, it flew to the other side of our extended kitchen/family room, but even then, it kept on staring at Jeannie through the patio window.

There was something profoundly spiritual about that cardinal on that cold winter day, and it touched Jeannie deeply. I was so moved when she told me the story over dinner, and so encouraged that Jeannie received God's love through that cardinal.

The Bible says we should consider the birds, and in His tender mercy, God used a cardinal to give another glimmer of love and light to Jeannie.

On another day, Jeannie was on her way out of the house and was prompted to take out Alex's suicide note. It had been at the back of her desk drawer since she first read it, on the night Alex took his life.

Shaking and trembling, Jeannie read the note once more. Grief welled up from within her, and slumping to the floor, she wept. Almost trance-like and crystal-clear, these words came to her mind: "Kick Satan in the teeth!"

Bringing the note into the light seemed to have brought about a paradigm shift in her thinking. Up to this point she had blamed God for what happened to Alex. Now she was blaming her adversary, Satan.

As she told me the story that night, my heart leaped within me, as I could see that Jeannie had taken a significant step forward. The battle would rage back and forth over the next few years, but a shift had happened in the spiritual realm. What Jeannie didn't know was that shortly after Alex passed, God had clearly spoken to me from the following Scripture:

> *The God of peace will soon crush Satan under your feet.*
> *The grace of our Lord Jesus be with you.*
>
> **Romans 16:20**

I experienced God's lovingkindness in bringing glimmers of light and love into Jeannie's dark and grieving heart.

I experienced the truth made clear in scripture that whatever darkness may come upon us, it cannot overcome the light of Christ within us. We often hear this Scripture in the season of Advent: The light shines in the darkness, and the darkness has not overcome it (John 1:5).

63.

More Pain and Suffering

In 2009, I was concerned when my brother Will told me he was having some pain in his groin. I was devastated when he was diagnosed with lung cancer a short time later. I prayed and wept. A few weeks later, I received a call from my brother Kim. Will had been taken to the hospital and only had a short time to live.

I took the first flight to France to be with my brother. I went straight to the hospital, where I met up with my mom and Kim. When we were allowed to, we stayed with Will in his room. He was thankful that I flew from America to be with him. He was heavily sedated with morphine, but every now and again he would wake up and we would have a brief conversation about all the good times we had.

Early in the morning of the third day, we got the call that Will was about to pass. We were all quiet on the way to the hospital. We arrived a short time before his last breath. Similar to when Jax died, his breathing got shallower and shallower, and then he was gone.

I'll never forget seeing my mom cuddle her son's head and sob and sob.

Because of what happened to Jax, I watched carefully when Will breathed his last breath. It was clear it was his last breath, because his head slumped down, and then, thirty seconds later, without inhaling, his lips blew out another breath. I believe God allowed me to see Will's spirit leave his body on its way to be with the Lord.

Before we left the hospital, the senior doctor pulled us aside and told us that in all his years in medicine, he had never seen anyone who knew they were going to die to have such peace as Will had.

Not long after Will went home to heaven, we received yet more bad news. Joshua, our 14 year-old nephew, had been hit and killed by a car!

Our hearts went out to Jeannie's brother Austin and his family. I had several conversations with Austin on the phone. We wept, and I prayed for him. He was grateful for the words of comfort that Jeannie and I gave him from our own journey of grief. In one of our calls, Austin received Jesus Christ as his Savior and his Lord.

64.

The Wedding Dance

Slowly, very slowly, Jeannie started coming back to me. One of my greatest joys was that we started to pray together. I had my best friend and prayer partner back.

Jeannie found great comfort in the Psalms. She read about the struggles David had and how he questioned God and cried out to Him for help and for answers. Jeannie's love for God's word was renewed and she started sharing Scriptures with me over dinner. I thanked God for this answer to my prayers and for the love and joy of the Lord I started to see in Jeannie's eyes and face.

Little by little, Jeannie's love for me was also restored. She allowed me to hold her hand when we walked the dogs, and we began having romantic evenings again.

Another glimmer of hope came at the wedding of the daughter of our friends George and Judy. Jeannie, Rebecca, and I were invited, and we were seated with the family.

It was truly a delightful wedding, and after the dinner and speeches, the guests joined the bride and groom on the dance floor. Rebecca and I danced for a short while, and I glanced over and saw Jeannie chatting with Dorothy, Judy's mother. I said to Rebecca, "Let's ask Mom to dance." Rebecca smiled in agreement, and we walked over to where Jeannie was sitting. It was a miracle that Jeannie was even at the wedding, but to get her to dance would be something else.

I held out my hand to Jeannie as a gesture, inviting her to dance with us. I could see Jeannie was a little overwhelmed. But she looked at my hand, and then up into my eyes, then glanced back to Dorothy, who with a nod of her head made it clear that she should dance with us. Jeannie placed her hand in mine, and the three of us danced together. Rebecca went to dance with someone else, leaving Jeannie and me twirling in the middle of the dance floor, with everyone nodding and smiling at us. The whole town had mourned and grieved with us over Alex's suicide, and this was the first time Jeannie had danced in eight years.

For eight years I had held on to the following Scripture:

You have turned my mourning into joyful dancing. You have taken away my clothes of mourning and clothed me with joy, that I might sing praises to you and not be silent. O LORD my God, I will give you thanks forever!

Psalm 30:11-12

Before my eyes, God answered my prayer and turned Jeannie's mourning into dancing!

I experienced again that God's Word is true and can be trusted.

65.

Unbelievable! Unthinkable! Unimaginable!

In 2014, Rebecca and I spoke at a conference in Southern California. I didn't know then that this would be the last time that I would stand next to my daughter. I watched her with such pride as she shone for Jesus in sharing about Alpha Youth. After the conference, Rebecca stayed for more speaking engagements and meetings. I also didn't know this would be my last hug with Rebecca before I left to meet up with Jeannie in Chicago. We then traveled to London for the Alpha leaders' conference, followed by visits to see Ben, friends and our moms.

Our moms both lived close to the South Downs, where Jeannie and I grew up. They lived in different villages, and to make the most of our time with them, we stayed with our respective moms.

I had just finished supper with my mom, and we were catching up when my cell phone rang.

"Hello," I said, wondering why someone would ring me so late.

"Hello, is that Mr. Long?" a man asked.

"Yes," I said. "Why do you ask?"

"Mr. Long, this is Inspector Steel from the Lake Forest police department, and I need to ask you—is your wife a runner?"

I thought it was strange for a police officer to be calling me to ask if Jeannie was a runner.

"No, my wife is not a runner, but my daughter is."

I continued, "What is this all about? Why do you need to know?"

"Mr. Long, I can't tell you now, but I will call you back later." And with that, he hung up.

I was dumbfounded. What a bizarre phone call! Straightaway, I called Rebecca's cell phone, but there was no answer. I tried again and again, but she wasn't picking up.

It was past 10 p.m. in the UK, and after a long day, I thought it would be best to let Jeannie sleep. I didn't want to trouble her with this strange call.

I waited with my mom for the officer to call me back. We prayed, and we waited, and we waited, but there was no call. I was getting very concerned. I called the Lake Forest police department and explained that I needed to hear back from Officer Steel. I told the person on the phone that I was in the UK, and it was after 11 p.m. The person took the message and said the officer would get back to me shortly.

The officer called me back a few minutes later, but he only added more confusion to the mystery by asking me more questions, such as, "Did Rebecca run in the Chicago 5K?"

We went back and forth a couple of times.

My tears are flowing now. Before I continue, I want you to know that I am struggling to write again.

He then said the unbelievable, unthinkable, and unimaginable, something a parent should never have to hear. And I was hearing it for a second time!

"Mr. Long," he said, "I'm sorry to have to tell you this, but a young woman has drowned in Lake Michigan, and we think it's your daughter Rebecca."

Silence—darkness.

I went into shock-numb. In the distance, I heard the officer say there was a key in the young woman's running shorts, and they wanted to see if it was for our house in Lake Forest. Weakly, I agreed.

I shared the news with my mom. She started to cry.

The officer called back a short time later and confirmed that the key was for our house.

He then said, "Mr. Long, I need you to identify Rebecca."

I stared at a photo of my daughter Rebecca. I stared and stared. I was speechless. I couldn't believe what was going on.

My mom couldn't stop sobbing, but I was too numb and shocked to cry.

Jeannie my precious Jeannie. Having watched her struggle for eight years to finally surface again after Alex's death, I didn't want to think about what this would do to her.

My mom and I decided it would be better to tell Jeannie in the morning, allowing her to have some much-needed sleep.

I didn't sleep much that night but as I lay there in the dark the tears came and I wept, and I called out to God for help. Looking back, I realize my unseen friend was always with me. He was with me in my pain and my tears. He carried me. Otherwise, how could I have kept going in those unbelievable days?

The next morning, we somberly drove over to share the unbelievable news with Jeannie. They were out when we arrived at my mother-in-law's apartment. The concierge let us in. We waited quietly for their return. It wasn't long. We heard them chatting and laughing in the hallway. The key turned, and in they came. Jeannie was delighted to see me.

But then she saw my face. I didn't have to say much.

"It's Rebecca..."

Jeannie collapsed into my arms as we fell to the floor in the depths of anguish, grieving for our beautiful daughter, Rebecca. The screams and the sobbing went on and on.

There is nothing more I can say. There just aren't words.

66.

Another Funeral

On the drive back to London for our flight home, we wept bitterly. The closer we got to London, the more I wept. My mind was filled with memories of happy days with Rebecca. We were all together then, but now we had two huge holes in our hearts.

Jeannie's heart was broken in pieces for a second time, and she wept uncontrollably for most of the trip back to the U.S.

I thank God for our friends Mark and Jenny, and David and Tina, who at just the right moment looked after us by making our trip back to the U.S. and our home in Lake Forest as comfortable as it could be. The love and support we felt from our friends after Rebecca went home to heaven truly was divine. It felt as though the Lord was hugging us and carrying us, and of course, He was.

I was surprised by the outpouring of grief. Men and women we hardly knew told us that when they heard the news about Rebecca, they wept. The messages poured in from all around the world, offering sincere condolences and telling us how Rebecca had touched their lives through her walk with Christ.

People wrote and called and visited, to tell us how Rebecca had profoundly impacted them. We heard story after story of how Rebecca had inspired them in their faith, how she had even prayed and advised a friend in her challenging marriage, and through her work as the Alpha USA youth director, how she had led so many young people to faith in Jesus. From the hundreds of messages these are a few that stood out to us:

"I thought of Rebecca's work in the U.S. and all around the world, and the lives that were and will continue to be impacted because of her faithfulness to serve Christ and others. I thought of all the seeds she had planted and how our tears in the grief of her loss will water those seeds and great fruit will arise because of her legacy."

"Rebecca had a lasting impact on my life. Never before had I met such a beautiful young lady who was also sold out for God. Her faith, kindness and strength in the midst of her own grief so impressed me that I renewed my faith and started teaching Sunday school in my local church."

"Rebecca is a role model of the type of woman I want to be. I became more inspired by her as I witnessed her unmatched faith. She helped me see what a young woman living for the Lord looks like and made me want to be like her."

As I write today, nearly six years on, my heart is so sad in not having our daughter with us!

Rebecca's funeral was held at Christ Church Lake Forest, the same as Alex's funeral some eight years before. Pastor Mike Woodruff welcomed us, and the service was led by our friend David. David's heart for the hurting shone through in how he cared for our family and friends in the midst of the immense grief.

The church was filled with friends and family from all around the world. Rebecca loved her school days, and some of her best friends from the UK came all the way to honor their friend.

Among the messages in the service, her friends wrote a sweet poem about Rebecca and their happy days together. Another friend sounded like an angel as she sang a song in memory of Rebecca.

Jeannie, almost fainting with sorrow, could hardly walk the long aisle toward Rebecca's coffin. With Ben helping his mother on one side and me on the other, we slowly made our way to our seats. With Alex and Rebecca having gone home ahead of us, we were now only three.

Jeannie's heart was crushed to pieces. She groaned and howled her way through the service, sounding like a wounded animal. Once was enough to hear Jeannie in such anguish, but a second time, was almost too much for me to bear. Ben sobbed his heart out. He had already lost his younger brother and now he lost his big sister. My heart broke for him.

We buried Rebecca's body next to Alex's in the Lake Forest cemetery. Our friends and family joined us at the grave site, and the grief poured forth as the sun cast shadows over the sad farewell. It seemed to me as though a river of love was flowing as we were hugged and kissed, each person wanting in some way to help us in our grief. I sensed the presence of the Lord. He reminded me that this was not the end—it was just the beginning. We thanked God for Rebecca and the gift she was to us and countless others.

We said au revoir—until we meet again.

67.

A Divine Encounter

The members of Christ Church were incredible. With meals, flowers, cards, messages, and so forth, they could not have done more to love and care for us.

It was quiet in our home.

After all that Jeannie had already endured, Rebecca's sudden death was too much for her to take. Sensing the darkness starting to overwhelm her, she knew she could not go on.

She decided to end her life.

Slowly, quietly, Jeannie walked upstairs to Rebecca's bedroom. She decided she wasn't going to come out.

Sometime later, she came downstairs.

I looked up from reading the Bible. I had one of those indescribable moments.

Jeannie looked different. Her face was radiant. She was almost glowing.

I went over to her, and looking into her now-sparkling eyes, I said,

"Jeannie, what has happened to you?"

"Gerard," she answered, "as I walked into Rebecca's room I was enveloped in light, and I fell on the floor. I experienced love that I had never felt before. It was as though time stood still. The air was sparkling with joy and I could breathe for the first time in eight years. God spoke to me, and one of the things He said was, 'Your grief is not your own.'"

I held Jeannie in my arms. We stood quietly, in what seemed like a sacred moment. I had wondered if Jeannie would even survive Rebecca's death, and suddenly, I had her back. I hugged her even closer. I thanked God from the bottom of my heart.

> *I experienced again that a short time in God's presence transforms a person, whatever they are going through.*

Season Eight—New Beginnings

Over the next few chapters, I'm going to tell you how God spoke to us and how He led us to our new beginning.

I couldn't get those profound words out of my mind: "Your grief is not your own." But what did they mean? We needed guidance.

At other times in our lives we had cried out to God to lead us, but this time, the cry was coming from our brokenness. God answered us.

I pray that our experience in hearing from God will give you knowledge and insight, as He guides you on your journey.

68.

"Behold, I Will Do a New Thing"

We memorize and meditate on God's Word, which is food for our soul, and we base our prayers on scripture. Before Jesus went to the cross, He prayed in the Garden of Gethsemane, "My Father, if it is possible, may this cup be taken from me. Yet not as I will, but as you will" (Matthew 26:39). We prayed, "Lord, we don't like the cup You have given us. It's so bitter, but if this is our calling, what do You want us to do with the brokenness You have placed in our hands?"

Jeannie and I were overwhelmed, but God gave us the courage and the strength to pray "not our will" and mean it.

At this time, our friends Bill and Jami invited Jeannie, Ben, and I to get away and have some time together at their home in Mexico. The timing was perfect, and we were so grateful to be still and to grieve in such a beautiful setting. Jeannie and I were able to pray and seek God's will for the next steps in our life.

The words of Isaiah the prophet kept coming to us:

Do not remember the former things, nor consider the things of old.
Behold, I will do a new thing, now it shall spring forth;
Shall you not know it? I will even make a
road in the wilderness and rivers in the desert.

Isaiah 43:18-19 (NKJV)

As we stepped out in faith, the "new thing" God had for us started to take shape.

As with other major changes of direction in our lives, we started to receive more and more confirmations that God was moving us on. Over the next few months, we received eighteen separate messages from people sharing a Scripture, a dream, a picture, or a prophecy that they believed were for us.

69.

Words from the Lord

The Lord had spoken to us, and we had clearly heard His voice over the years through the Bible and by the Holy Spirit (1 Corinthians 6:19; 2 Corinthians 6:16). His Word had come to us directly and through other people, and He had often spoken to us through His creation.

It's humbling to think that the Creator of the universe would speak to us, but He does, and these are some of the words we received from May to October 2014:

The daughter of a friend of Jeannie was deeply moved by our grief. She had never received a prophetic word before. She shared various words and pictures she believed God had given her for Jeannie and me. It took her several months to gain the courage to share these words with us. Here's what she told us (my comments in italics):

God is going to use Jeannie in a powerful way (*people often say how powerfully Jeannie speaks*);

Gerard's time with Alpha USA is coming to an end, and he will start a nonprofit and share God's word around the world (*this happened at the end of 2014, and our social media messages reach millions of people around the world*);

There is going to be a resurrection (*I died for thirty minutes on October 26, 2019*);

There was a picture of an airplane window and a missile starting a war (*I think this speaks of the isolation and travel ban, caused by the war on COVID-19*).

She said she felt that, "God did not want to allow this. It's like He kept pushing back when this would happen, it pained Him so much. He is heartbroken for you. He did it because it was so important. He watched with head down...and the palm of His hand was on His forehead."

The last part of the prophecy was profound and meant a lot to me. It was a strong confirmation of what I had seen—the Lord was suffering with us.

God never causes evil, but sometimes He permits it for a greater eternal purpose. God is a God of love, and He hates suffering. He sees and knows all the pain we go through. When someone yields to God's call to 'take up their cross' and surrender to God's will, the life of Jesus shines through that person as a witness to other people. The following Scriptures now mean so much to me:

We always carry around in our body the death of Jesus, so that the life of Jesus may also be revealed in our body. For we who are alive are always being given over to death for Jesus' sake, so that his life may also be revealed in our mortal body. So then, death is at work in us, but life is at work in you...All this is for your benefit, so that the grace that is reaching more and more people may cause thanksgiving to overflow to the glory of God.

2 Corinthians 4:10-12, 15

It's a paradox but the Bible teaches that it is a calling and privilege to suffer for Christ and His kingdom (Philippians 1:29).

Nick and Jo, two of our closest friends in England who pastored the church in London with us, prayed with us in May 2014. Nick had the following picture and word for us. He saw a flock of geese flying in a V formation. The goose at the front dropped back, and another goose took its place. He felt it was time for me to step down from the Alpha USA role because God had another assignment for me.

Several of our friends, including two of the Alpha USA board members, told us that they believed God had another work for me to do.

Several friends shared Isaiah 61:1-4 with us. These became the founding Scriptures for our new ministry:

The Spirit of the Sovereign LORD is on me, because the LORD has anointed me to proclaim good news to the poor. He has sent me to bind up the brokenhearted, to proclaim freedom for the captives and release from darkness for the prisoners, to proclaim the year of the LORD's favor and the day of vengeance of our God, to comfort all who mourn, and provide for those who grieve in Zion—to bestow on them a crown of beauty instead of ashes, the oil of joy instead of mourning, and a garment of praise instead of a spirit of despair. They will be called oaks of righteousness, a planting of the LORD for the display of his splendor. They will rebuild the ancient ruins and restore the places long devastated; they will renew the ruined cities that have been devastated for generations.

We also had clear indications that God wanted us to move from our home in Lake Forest, but we had no idea where He wanted us to go.

I had a strong sense that there was going to be another awakening that would sweep around the world like an enormous tsunami. I had a picture in my office of a huge wave that was about to break over a field of wheat. Spiritual awakenings have occurred throughout history when the presence of God comes and people become aware of their need to repent and get right with Him. Examples include the Welsh Awakening in 1904, Azusa Street in Los Angeles from 1906 to 1909, and several "Great Awakenings" in America from the eighteenth century through the twentieth century.

After Jeannie's encounter and transformation, the Lord also spoke to her about the wave. The same day, Jeannie's prayer partner Jenny sent her a picture of a surfer riding a wave.

Shortly after, I was invited to speak in Malibu, California. While we were there, our friend Lani, who had been on Rebecca's Alpha Youth USA board, put us up in the Malibu Beach Inn.

On the day we arrived, I had to go to a meeting, but when I got back to the hotel room, I found Jeannie in tears.

"Darling, what's wrong?" I asked.

"I'm missing our children, and I feel bewildered, but I want to tell you something the Lord is showing me," she answered. "I just found a picture in this magazine, and it's the exact same picture I have kept with my papers for the last few years.

"I've just noticed, the picture is of a woman looking out over the ocean from a beach house in Malibu. I had never read the tiny print before."

Jeannie continued, "I've been watching the surfers riding the waves, and then I noticed from the hotel information that the beach is called Surf-Rider Beach."

This was all such a confirmation of the picture Jenny sent. We had to be ready and patient to catch the wave God had for us.

While we were in Malibu, Lani arranged several opportunities for me to speak and tell our story. One was a lunch in memory of Rebecca. A lady we had never met before started to tell me some words she believed God had given her when she was praying for us. She began speaking about a huge wave that was coming and that we were supposed to get on the wave like surfers. At this point, I asked the lady to stop, and I called Jeannie over to listen to what she was saying. It was such an encouragement, confirming what the Lord had already said to us.

At another event, two people said they felt God was calling us to move to Malibu. The next day, another person also said they felt God wanted us to be in Malibu, California.

> *I experienced again how powerful and helpful it is to receive prophetic words to help discern the path God had planned for us.*

70.

Suffering as a Calling

From all the words we received, I knew there was a major change coming, but Jeannie and I wanted to know what this meant for us. What did God want us to do? Where would we be based? Most importantly, would our son Ben want to join us?

As we prayed, we felt God wanted us to use what He had placed in our hands. To us it was brokenness! But not just this—we had also experienced God's grace in giving us comfort, hope, and strength to journey on. We were in a unique position to minister to the suffering, to connect through empathy, and to share the wonderful truth of God's grace. If He can rescue us in all that we had been through, He can rescue anyone!

The words that the Lord spoke to Jeannie in her encounter with God in Rebecca's bedroom—"Your grief is not your own"—were a great help in understanding God's new call on our lives.

One day our stories will all make perfect sense. Until then, we believe God is calling us to take what Satan had intended to destroy us with and turn it around to help others.

The following Scripture came alive to us:

Who comforts us in all our troubles, so that we can comfort those in any trouble with the comfort we ourselves receive from God.

2 Corinthians 1:4

We pondered these words: "The person who can comfort and give hope to the suffering is the one who has known suffering." And the one who can best minister to a broken heart is the one who has known a broken heart.

Jeannie and I were stepping out in faith, one step at a time, believing the Lord was calling us to a new thing—a new ministry and a new location in Malibu, California. We were being called to help people who were suffering in the U.S. and around the world.

We had made several major moves in our lives, including the transfer from London to New York, and we knew this next one was not going to be easy. Stepping out in faith, we had peace in the knowledge that this was God's will and He was with us.

The hardest thing about the move involved Ben. He had moved to the U.S. from the UK to be with us and had started to do some contract work for Alpha USA. We prayed and tried to persuade Ben to come with us to Malibu, but he wanted to stay with his new friends in Chicago. We took comfort in Ben's assurance that he would join us at a later date.

I was going to miss my friends and colleagues at Alpha USA. We were like a family, and we had poured so much of our lives into the ministry over the previous eight years. The staff all knew and loved Rebecca, and we had been on the road of tragedy and grief together. We received several words of encouragement for the next part of our journey, and the Alpha USA board was very supportive. When the day came to say goodbye, there were more tears, but I had peace in my heart. We were being obedient to our calling, to move into the next chapter of our lives.

A friend said to us, "All that has happened in your lives to date was to prepare you for your next assignment. This is the big one." I believed this was true.

Every direction we turned, Isaiah 61 kept coming back to us. Jesus quoted the first two verses of Isaiah 61 when He started His public ministry.

"The Spirit of the Lord is on me," He said, "because He has anointed me to preach good news to the poor. He has sent me to heal the brokenhearted, to proclaim freedom for the captives and release from darkness for the prisoners."

And, the Lord had used verse three to encourage me when He was healing Jeannie after Alex went home to heaven:

To all who mourn in Israel, He will give a crown of beauty for ashes, a joyous blessing instead of mourning, festive praise instead of despair. In their righteousness, they will be like great oaks that the LORD has planted for his own glory.

I have found that an effective way to reach people who don't yet know Christ, is to share God's love with the poor, the brokenhearted, the captives, and the prisoners.

The best way to connect with people is through suffering. Suffering gives you the special gift of empathy, the ability to offer comfort and hope to those gripped by pain and darkness, because you have traveled the same road. This is what Jesus did for us, He emptied Himself and visited humankind to empathize with us in all that we go through (Hebrews 4:15).

With many tears, but also with anticipation and stirrings of hope, we launched Awakening to God Ministries (ATG). Through it we would share God's amazing grace and we would remember and honor the lives of Rebecca and Alex.

First planted in our hearts during our encounters with God, our prayer was for everyone to have an awakening to God's glory—His wonderful love and His unimaginable beauty and majesty—and to have an awakening to God's unique call on every person's life to fulfill their purpose through the good and the bad times. Our ministry would be to share God's love by giving comfort and hope to the poor, the brokenhearted, the captives, and the prisoners.

The logo for ATG is the number eight turned on its side—the sign for infinity. We came up with this logo because Alex and Rebecca both passed on the eighth of the month, eight years apart, and eight hundred feet from each other, on the same beach. They were both 800-meter runners. The number eight in the Bible signifies new beginnings, which is what we believed God was doing. He was doing a new thing (see Isaiah 43:18-19), and because nothing is impossible for God, the potential is infinite—limitless.

We knew it would be impossible to run ATG in our own strength. It would have to be by God's grace alone. His grace has come to us in various ways. We know we would never have made it this far without the prayers, love, and financial support of our friends. In particular, some (you know who you are) have loved and embraced us as family. And so it has been.

> *Once again, I experienced God's grace guiding me by the hand of my Good Shepherd, leading me along the path of my purpose and empowering me to do the work prepared for me.*

71.

The Call to Malibu

Following our hearts and the directions we felt God had given us, on a crisp, clear February morning in 2015, we packed as much as we could fit into our car for our calling to Malibu.

Jeannie wept as we hugged and kissed Ben goodbye in our driveway. I said a prayer asking God to watch over him and us on our travels. We waved to him as I watched him disappear from view in the rear-view mirror. And we clung to the hope that he would join us later.

Our guardian angels worked overtime on our trip. We traveled through a freak storm with snow and ice on the road and a stone hitting our windshield. The closer we got to California, the more we felt an unseen opposition. As we approached Malibu, we came close to having a major accident. It was as if Satan was determined to stop us from taking up our next assignment.

At the end of the three-day, 2,300-mile trip, we were exhausted, but we gave thanks to the Lord that we had arrived in one piece. We arrived to a beautiful sunset.

We were thankful to have three days to recover in the beach house of our friends David and Tina. We had no idea where we would live, but as always, the Lord provided. Lani had a sister who came to the rescue by allowing us to stay for a few days in her quaint beach house overlooking one of the surfing spots in Malibu. As we watched the surfers riding the huge rolling waves, it seemed as though the Lord was reminding us that we too had to wait for the right wave—His wave, for the next part of our journey.

Very few rentals allowed dogs, but after praying, we found a 12-month rental home on Malibu Road. It was a first-floor apartment that was right on the beach with a view of both the sunrise and the sunset. How grateful we were to find such a beautiful place for Jeannie and me to heal! I loved the sound of the waves and the fresh ocean air filled our lungs. Every day we walked hand in hand on the beach, chatting, crying, and praying, and throwing tennis balls for our golden retrievers, Chelsea and Chloe.

18 months before we even knew we would move to Malibu, our friend Judy had a dream of us living in an apartment overlooking the beach with a garden in the back. George and Judy came to visit us, and Judy confirmed that our apartment was the place she had seen in her dream.

Shortly before moving out of our rental on Malibu Road, Chelsea suddenly became ill. Her kidneys were failing, and Lani helped us to do all we could to save her. Sadly, it was not to be, and we had to make the heartbreaking decision to put her down. With tears streaming down her cheeks, Jeannie said farewell to Chelsea. Looking out for her to the end, Chelsea lifted her paw and put it over Jeannie's hand.

72.

Sharing the Story

Our friends had often told us that we needed to tell our story. Shortly after arriving in Malibu, a number of developments pointed to the possibility of doing a film of our story.

Lani suddenly announced, "Your film will be the big one." God had placed Lani in an influential position in the film industry, and we were surprised and encouraged by her comment.

Around the same time as Lani's announcement, a man I hardly knew emailed me with an introduction to someone named Ted. He said that we needed to meet. I reached out to Ted—who turned out to be Ted Baehr, founder of MovieGuide.com and The Christian Film & Television Commission. Over lunch with him and his daughter, Jeannie and I discovered that for many years he had been working and praying for God's kingdom to come to Hollywood.

We told our story, and besides being deeply moved, Ted said, "This has got to be a film!" As a next step, he suggested I attend his scriptwriters' course, which was starting in two weeks.

We thanked Ted for his encouragement, but when we discovered the course cost $1,400, we didn't think we could afford it. We handed it over to the Lord, praying, "Lord, if You want me to do this course, please provide the funds."

A few days later, some new friends invited me to tell our story with a small number of their friends. About 25 people came to their ranch-style house in the mountains. At the end of my talk, my friend suggested they take up an offering for Jeannie and me. I was grateful and flabbergasted when Jeannie and I discovered that the offering came to exactly $1,400.

I signed up for Ted's scriptwriting course and found it immensely helpful. I was fascinated to discover that films usually follow a structure that was first established by William Shakespeare.

The more I listened and learned, the more I felt the story that God had given us was almost tailor-made for a film. Every night I would eagerly share with Jeannie the things I had learned, and at the end of the course, with Ted's encouragement, it seemed right to start working on a script.

A friend of mine had recently been appointed the chief operating officer of Pureflix, a Christian version of Netflix, and he encouraged me to finish the script.

Over the next few months, we had several more confirmations, including planned and unplanned meetings with influential movie makers who lived only two miles from us in Malibu.

We also had two unusual meetings.

Jeannie and I were invited to several film premieres. At one of these, I was introduced to a guy who is one of the main Christian film distributors in the U.S. After the normal introductions, the man stepped back and said, "You're not Rebecca Long's dad, are you?"

"Yes, I am," I answered.

The man then turned to a colleague and said, "Rebecca was one of the most holy women I have ever met."

He stepped forward and said to me, "I'm so sorry for your loss, but I have to say, Rebecca was such a holy woman. I met her in Southern California in early May, 2014 and when I heard the tragic news about her passing, I wasn't that surprised. It was as though she was walking so close to the Lord, it was an easy step into heaven!" He went on, "If there is ever anything I can do for you, please don't hesitate to ask me."

It was humbling and sad to hear the man's recollection of our daughter, whom we so missed.

At another premiere, out of maybe five hundred seats, I ended up sitting next to a guy who had known Rebecca when she was running Alpha Youth. He was currently running Campus Renewal and was keen to help us with our film. At the end of the premiere, he introduced us to the chief executive officer of Pureflix.

We had several other meetings with people in the movie industry, and believed more and more that God wanted our story to be told through film. I started to plan the structure of the story. We had lots of fun imagining who might play our parts.

I worked hard on the script through the summer of 2015 and sent the finished version to Ted's editing team for review. To my pleasant surprise, they gave it an A minus.

My friend Bob arranged for a major Christian film company to review our script and discuss it with us. We were shocked when they told us our story would fit into the horror genre, and they were not interested. We felt he had totally missed the message of the story, which is love triumphing over evil, redeeming others held captive to suffering.

Through the disappointment, and after praying, we knew it was not the right time for our movie. Our story would be told through film but at a later date.

Jeannie and I left the movie in God's hands and concentrated on building the ATG ministry.

> *I have learned the importance of waiting on God's timing for a vision to be fulfilled.*

73.

Touches from God

At times in my life I have received what I call a touch from God. This might be a powerful sense of His presence, or it could be an event that some might call a coincidence.

I have learned that the closer you get to God, the more you see Him in your day.

While we were living in Malibu, we had several touches from God that encouraged our hearts and let us know He was near. I hope you will be encouraged by what I'm about to tell you, not only what happened but also the timing of the event.

A Whale's Breach

I started doing live ATG Facebook channel video talks on the beach early every morning. I spoke a few words using the daily Scripture on our app, ATG Today (www.atgtoday.com), and ended with prayer.

One morning, the memory Scripture was:

When I consider your heavens, the work of your fingers, the moon and the stars, which you have set in place, what is mankind that you are mindful of them, human beings that you care for them?

Psalms 8:3-4

Because I love God's creation, I was getting quite animated this particular morning, speaking out loud God's praises and declaring His wonders and glory. I said a closing prayer, switched off the video, and turned to look out over the ocean. Just as I turned around, I saw a surging in the water, and then a huge whale breached, about a hundred yards out from where I was standing. It was so close, I could see its body, and as it dived down, its tail came out of the water, and then it disappeared under the waves. The bracing smell of the ocean, the explosive spray from the crashing waves, and the unexpected sight of the whale left me marveling at God's incredible creation. My heart swelled with gratitude for His great love for me.

In the four years Jeannie and I lived on this particular beach, this was the only whale I ever saw. The whale breached exactly in line with where I was standing, and it happened immediately after I had finished sharing about God's glory in creation. As you can imagine, over breakfast I was excited to share with Jeannie my encounter with the whale, and we both thanked God for His creation.

Hearts on the Beach

Jeannie and I never ceased to praise and thank God for letting us heal on one of the most magnificent beaches in America. One of the highlights of our day was our morning walk along the beach. As the mighty waves rolled in like galloping white horses, we felt the spray on our faces and breathed in the fresh ocean air. Hand in hand, we would walk and talk and pray, laugh and cry, and give thanks and praise to God for His lovingkindness to us.

If Jeannie wasn't with me, I would try to bring her back a striking shell or stone. One of Jeannie's favorites was any stone in the shape of a heart.

We miss our children every day, but some days are harder than others.

Once, Jeannie decided to skip our morning walk, preferring to be on her own. About half a mile into my walk, I noticed a stone buried in the sand but clear enough to see it was in the shape of a heart. I picked up the stone, cleaned it off, and realized it was no ordinary stone. This was a magnificent pink piece of cut marble in the shape of a heart, and despite being in the sand, it was smooth!

When I arrived home, I asked Jeannie to close her eyes and hold out her hands. I placed the unusual stone in her soft hands. She could feel the smooth marble stone, but when she opened her eyes and saw that its shape was of a beautiful heart, tears started to fall down her face.

God had allowed me to find an exquisitely carved marble heart on the morning that Jeannie was particularly missing Rebecca.

On another occasion, I was walking on the beach with our dog Chloe and my friend Steve, with his dog Arthur. The day before, Jeannie and I were both grieving, as we remembered Rebecca on what would have been her 37th birthday. Close to the place where I had found the pink marble heart, I spotted not one but three more marble hearts. Steve asked if he could have one of the hearts to give to his daughter, and I kept the other two. One was pink, and the other was green, Alex's favorite color.

Once again, when I arrived home, I asked Jeannie to close her eyes and hold out her hands. I placed a gift in both of her hands.

We both marveled at God's kindness to allow me to find two more marble hearts on the day after Rebecca's birthday—one each in remembrance of Rebecca and Alex.

Rainbow Mouth

Every morning after breakfast, Jeannie and I prayed, worshiped and gave thanks to the Lord. One morning, I was sharing about our desire to declare God's amazing grace in and through our journey of suffering. Suddenly, Jeannie stopped me and told me a rainbow had formed exactly on my mouth.

Clearly, the rainbow had been formed by the sun reflecting off an image somewhere, but we were both encouraged by this strange reflection, just as I was talking about wanting to share God's grace. We received this sign as an encouragement from the Lord. In the Bible, God gave the rainbow as a sign of His promise to never send another global flood, and we took the rainbow on my mouth as a promise that more doors would open in the future to share the living hope that He had placed in our hearts.

A $5 Bill

It was a particularly beautiful sunrise, and the beach was deserted. About a mile into our walk, I spotted a $5 bill just sitting on top of the sand. As I picked it up, Jeannie spoke out a simple prayer.

"Oh, Lord," she said, "please multiply this $5 note a thousand times over."

The next day, we received a check in the mail. It was for $5,000, a fantastic gift for the work of ATG! As we saw the amount on the check, a huge surge of joy welled up from within us, and with laughter and praise to God, we did a little dance around our apartment.

Having walked thousands of miles, we had never before found a bank note on a beach.

We thanked God for the $5 on the beach, for Jeannie's prayer for a thousand times increase, and for the $5,000 check we received the next day. I should mention, on average, we probably receive a $5,000 check for ATG about once per year.

As we pondered this unusual event, Jeannie commented with a chuckle, "What a shame I didn't think to pray for a million times increase of the $5 note."

Manna from Heaven

ATG is a not-for-profit organization that is largely funded by gifts from generous donors. Mostly, these are people who know and love us and believe in the mission and vision of ATG to bring comfort and hope to the suffering.

Prayer is the most important part of ATG, and as I'm writing this, we have more than a hundred prayer partners, people who are committed to pray for us and who are willing to be called upon for any urgent prayer needs. Jeannie and I regularly pray for ATG, and one request is, "Oh Lord, please put ATG on people's hearts for prayer and financial support."

We had been asking the Lord for more finances to grow ATG, and we had been praying the prayer of Jabez:

Jabez cried out to the God of Israel, "Oh, that you would bless me and enlarge my territory! Let your hand be with me, and keep me from harm so that I will be free from pain." And God granted his request.

1 Chronicles 4:10

Jeannie particularly had it on her heart to see more zeroes in the gifts. Over the next three days, we had a growing sense that something big was about to drop into our lap.

We decided to visit our favorite outdoor mall in Malibu to buy some juice. It was another beautiful day, and we were strolling hand in hand under some trees when, for the first time in my life, a bird pooped on me! We're not superstitious, but jokingly, Jeannie said,

"Maybe that's a sign that God is about to do something big. After all, He often uses animals in the Bible."

The next day, we opened the mail, and there it was, the largest single gift that had ever been given to ATG. There were several zeroes after the number! Jeannie and I nearly fell off our stools. With tears in our eyes, we did a little praise dance, thanking the Lord for answering our prayers.

74.

A Battle Indeed

One of the secrets of our lasting marriage is that every day we pray together and intentionally declare the promises of God, resisting the schemes of our adversary, Satan. God's Word gives strength and joy to our weary hearts, as we seek to honor Him in our lives. We love to inspire and encourage each other with the stories in the Bible.

The story of Job is devastating, but because it's in the Bible, it has given Jeannie and me encouragement and hope in the crucible. In our battles, it has helped us to understand that ultimately, God is sovereign over our lives and Satan is only able to attack us within the boundaries God has set. In every attack on our lives, God is with us in the battle, and our story will have a good ending.

We are told

In the land of Uz there lived a man whose name was Job. This man was blameless and upright; he feared God and shunned evil.

Job 1:1

The narrative goes on to tell us that Job had a blessed family of ten children, and he was extremely wealthy.

He was the greatest man among all the people of the East.

Job 1:3

We are then given a glimpse into the workings of heaven. We are told that Job is the boast of heaven. One day, when the angels came to present themselves before the Lord, Satan is asked,

Have you considered my servant Job? There is no one on earth like him; he is blameless and upright, a man who fears God and shuns evil.

Job 1:8

We then listen in on a dialogue between Satan and the Lord. Satan claims that Job only honors God because He had put a hedge of protection around Job and had blessed him so much.

"But now," said Satan, "stretch out your hand and strike everything he has, and he will surely curse you to your face."

Job 1:11

Taking up the challenge, God allowed Satan to strike Job. One disaster after another befalls him, including the tragic death of his children and loss of all his wealth and possessions. In all his affliction, Job never cursed God. Instead, he said these words:

Naked I came from my mother's womb, and naked I will depart. The LORD gave and the LORD has taken away; may the name of the LORD be praised.

Job 1:21

However, Job's trials were not over. On another day, when God was boasting about Job, Satan said Job would soon curse God if his health was taken from him. Once again, Satan is given permission to attack Job. This time it's with an illness that covers his body in painful sores.

Job is in the eye of the storm. On top of this, three of his friends try to persuade him that all his trouble must have happened because he sinned against God. Job claims his innocence, but he is tormented by his suffering and the constant accusations of his so-called friends.

In all his trials, Job never cursed God, although he did have some questions as to why God allowed all his suffering. I so relate to Job because, like him, in my darkest hours, I cried out to God, "Why did You allow Satan to attack me and my family?" Tears well up even as I write these words.

At the end of the story, God never answered Job's questions, but He did ask Job to consider His creation and His sovereignty. Job is humbled, saying,

My ears had heard of you but now my eyes have seen you. Therefore, I despise myself and repent in dust and ashes.
Job 42:5-6

There is an encouraging end to the story, because the Lord restored Job's fortunes and gave him twice as much as he had before. Twice as many sheep, camels, oxen, and donkeys. Interestingly, God gave him the same number of children, because his other children were waiting for him in heaven. Truly, this is one of Jeannie's favorite Scriptures. As you can imagine, the end of Job's story is incredibly encouraging to Jeannie and me.

I'm overwhelmed with hope and joy as I anticipate seeing Rebecca and Alex again in heaven.

In the mystery of my own story, people have told us that I am like a modern-day Job.

Similar to the story of Job, two of our three children died in bizarre and catastrophic circumstances. Deep inside, we believed that surely, enough is enough in terms of any more battles for our faith.

In our affliction, Jeannie and I were grateful for God's grace to sustain us, to give us each other and our beloved son Ben, our loving and generous friends, and our good health and finances. But, in 2019, we found ourselves in the midst of another fierce battle, this time over our finances and our health.

Most of our savings were invested in our home in Lake Forest. In the short term, we were renting out the home and using the rental income to pay for our Malibu apartment. In the long term, we were planning to sell the house and release our savings.

The remainder of our personal finances were invested in a friend's residential property business in West Chicago. It was a great business, consisting of buying up large residential apartment blocks, restoring them, thereby increasing the property value and occupancy rates. My friend was a partner in ATG, was serving in two influential churches in Chicago, and supported some great Christian outreach within his apartment blocks. I had known him for several years, and I trusted him.

At the beginning of 2019, we received some shocking news.

First, our tenants in Lake Forest stopped paying the rent and even stole some of our possessions. Then we received more bad news. The property values were dropping in Lake Forest, and all our equity was wiped out, preventing us from selling our home. This was highly unusual. Prices were plummeting in the affluent Lake Forest area, but other areas on the North Shore of Chicago were red hot.

As if things couldn't get any worse with our finances, I was shocked to hear that my friend had made some unwise decisions and was being investigated by the Securities and Exchange Commission. It went from bad to worse as later in the year, all of his business assets were frozen, including our investment.

Jeannie and I viewed our money as a gift from God that needed to be used wisely. We tithed and found joy in giving to other ministries and individuals. We cried out to God to help us in this new battle of faith over our finances.

Similar to the story of Job, the battle got even worse when our health suddenly failed us.

All our lives, Jeannie and I had been fit and healthy. From the days when Jeannie was a ballerina and I was a middle-distance runner, we lived a healthy lifestyle and were in great shape. Apart from Jeannie's intestines knotting from the overwhelming grief of Alex's suicide, we had never had a serious illness or even been in the hospital. In forty years, apart from annual physicals, we had rarely visited a doctor.

In the past, we had medical insurance, but when we arrived in California, we researched our options and discovered we could only have insurance through the Affordable Care Act, which had monthly premiums of $1,500. This would have been a significant part of our income at the time. Because we were healthy and our medical needs were being met, either in the UK or with a national health study that I was part of, we decided not to take out any health insurance.

Obviously, after my cardiac arrest, we were badly affected by our decision.

I had been planning to take out a catastrophic insurance policy, but I was too late.

When I had my cardiac arrest, with no insurance coverage, we were suddenly facing medical bills of more than $100,000, and for the first time in our lives, we had no money to pay them. Plus, we had no tenants for our home in Lake Forest, and we were getting behind with our mortgage payments.

On top of everything else, I was facing a major battle over our finances. It was crystal-clear to me that Satan was behind the attack, and on one occasion, it became so obvious that I had to laugh in the face of the adversity. I took a call from an aggressive debt collector from the bank while on my way to a heart rehab session, who even threatened foreclosure on our home unless I sent some money.

Incredibly, despite the financial pressure and having to recover from the cardiac arrest, I had peace.

> *I experienced God's grace, and the wonderful love, support, and prayers of our friends and family were sustaining Jeannie and me.*

75.

The Battle After a Battle

As often happens when you are in a season of testing, there was more to come.

Over the previous two years, Jeannie had symptoms indicating that something was wrong with her bladder. Several times she saw a doctor, but each time, after blood work and urine tests, they told her she was fine and not to worry. But the symptoms did not go away, and Jeannie lost her peace. On the next visit to the doctor, she insisted on seeing a urologist.

On December 5, 2019, only six weeks after my cardiac arrest, I joined Jeannie in the urologist's office. We held hands and listened intently as the doctor explained what she had discovered in Jeannie's bladder.

I'll never forget the moment when I heard her say that Jeannie had bladder cancer.

I was unsure how Jeannie would react, but when our eyes met, I could see God's peace on her face. She later told me that it gave her peace to have me by her side, but she was concerned how my heart would take the bad news. It felt as though we were both being supernaturally carried in the moment.

I experienced His power and peace in the midst of another storm. "I am with you always" is a promise of His presence. But, it's not an undertaking to do it all for us!

With some close friends, we talked and prayed about our financial needs for Jeannie's upcoming surgery. God answered our prayers, and we managed to establish health insurance for 2020 within a two-week window.

We needed to find the best urologist. After recommendations from friends, Dr. Chamie accepted Jeannie as a patient, but he was fully booked for surgeries weeks in advance. On one particular day, I had a strong feeling that I should call Dr. Chamie's office, and we were over the moon to hear there had been a cancellation. We booked Jeannie there and then, and she had her tumors removed on January 8, 2020. As it turned out, the timing was perfect because, in removing the tumors, they discovered a serious infection that was about to flare up in Jeannie's bladder.

A few weeks later, we received the pathology results on the tumors.

"I have bad news and good news," Dr. Chamie announced. "The bad news is that the cancer is very aggressive." Hearing this news felt like a punch to my stomach. I was eager for the good news.

"The good news is that there is no evidence that the cancer has spread, and it looks as though we caught it all with the surgery."

Something didn't add up.

"If the cancer was very aggressive, and if it has been around for two years, judging by the blood in Jeannie's urine, how come it didn't spread?" I asked Dr. Chamie.

He shrugged his shoulders and said, "I guess some people just get lucky."

Jeannie and I glanced at each other and smiled, knowing that this was not luck but the mercy and grace of our heavenly Father.

Although Dr. Chamie could find no evidence of cancer in Jeannie's bladder, she still needed to follow the protocol of six weekly and ten monthly chemotherapy treatments. Every three months, she had to have a cystoscopy to check that her bladder was still clear. After each treatment, Jeannie was severely weakened for a few days but mercifully, with bladder cancer, one's hair does not fall out.

By March 2020, after reeling from Jeannie's health scare and treatment, I had to have a stent placed in another of the arteries supplying blood to my heart. I chose to be awake during the procedure, and strangely, it took a lot longer than I had been told to expect. Thinking that Satan wanted me dead, I prayed and asked God to bring the procedure to an end. My prayer was answered; the procedure came to a swift end, and I was allowed to go home that night.

In the early hours of the morning, I blacked out for the first time in my life. I collapsed in the bathroom and narrowly escaped cracking my skull against the sink. I was on blood thinners, and a blow to the head could have been fatal. Hearing an almighty crash, Jeannie jumped out of bed and ran to the bathroom. Finding me lying on the floor, she called 911. They rushed me to the hospital in an ambulance and I spent another night in the ICU. I had an allergic reaction to the dye they had been pumping into my heart during the procedure the day before. Thankfully, I recovered quickly.

Everything was going well, and we told our moms that we planned to be with them for Christmas. But, after Jeannie had nine chemotherapy treatments, we were given the upsetting news that the cancer had returned.

We were surprised and very disappointed with this news, and once again, with our prayer partners, we cried out to God for more grace to fight the cancer.

On September 2, Dr. Chamie successfully removed six more tumors from Jeannie's bladder, and after further checks, he said there was no more evidence of cancer.

Over the next few months, Jeannie had more chemotherapy treatments, more cystoscopies, and more tumors removed from her bladder—one on my birthday.

Jeannie had one final chemotherapy treatment, and we are now trusting that by God's grace, she will remain cancer-free.

The battle for my health continued when I developed an irregular heartbeat that needed to be treated. On January 25, 2021, I had a heart ablation, that eliminated my irregular heartbeat, and I soon recovered full fitness.

We don't know why some people suffer more than others, but I have a living hope that has helped to preserve me and keep me strong in the battles. My hope is an anchor for my soul in the knowledge that God is with me and He will never leave me. Even when you think all hope is lost, it never is—not really! God's Word is living and active in our lives, and this verse has proved to be true to me through many battles:

Fear not, for I am with you; Be not dismayed, for I am your God. I will strengthen you, yes, I will help you, I will uphold you with My righteous right hand.

Isaiah 41:10 NKJV

The health and finances portion of our story testifies to God's love and grace, too, just like all others aspects of our lives.

> *In the mystery of suffering, I have learned to have peace in the midst of the violent attacks on our health and our finances! I can confidently say in all circumstances, "It is well with my soul."*

> *I have learned that when disappointments come, it's an opportunity to experience Jesus' life at a deeper level—His patient endurance.*

76.

Garden of Eden

The Lord is preparing a table for us in the presence of our enemies, and He has shown us part of this in how He has cared for us in our battles.

When we arrived in Malibu, the Lord bonded us with a couple, Kris and Kimby, and their four children, Savannah, AJ, Carmel, and Summer.

Jeannie and I first met with Kris and Kimby at a juice bar. Kimby was eager to show Jeannie something in the bar, and when Jeannie saw what it was, she started to cry. It was the Bible reference Psalm 103:1-5, the last words that Alex had spoken to Jeannie before his suicide.

We went back to Kris and Kimby's home, and they showed us a huge painting in their bedroom. It was of a massive wave that was about to break—the same image God had given us for several years. For the next two hours we shared our stories, including the struggle they had following the birth of their only son, AJ, with severe cerebral palsy. We prayed and wept with them, and our hearts were bonded in suffering and in the hope of seeing another awakening.

Over the next few years, we met with Kris and Kimby on Friday nights to worship the Lord and to pray for an awakening, and I would share a teaching from the Bible. We loved to follow the pattern of Shabbat Shalom, which is the Jewish tradition of welcoming the Sabbath for rest and renewal.

Their whole family loved our dog Chloe, and they looked after her while we were on our travels. They were so impressed by Chloe and the fun she brought to their family that they bought their own golden puppy, whom they appropriately named Hope. Hope and Chloe became friends, and we had great fun looking after both dogs and AJ while they were away.

Kris is like a spiritual son to me, and we often prayed and had fellowship together. We started a weekly men's prayer meeting in Kris's office. Kris is a man of God with a great heart, and I was touched when I heard that he had wept when he heard about my cardiac arrest.

Throughout our convalescing, Kris and Kimby came alongside us and went the second mile in allowing us to stay in their coach house. We could not have been in a more beautiful place; we called it the Garden of Eden. We were surrounded by gardens that had an abundance of singing birds and lots of other wildlife. Every morning, we looked up in awe at the majestic Santa Monica mountains and were reminded of one of our favorite Scriptures:

I lift up my eyes to the mountains—where does my help come from? My help comes from the LORD, the Maker of heaven and earth.

Psalm 121:1-2

We also had access to one of the most idyllic private beaches in Malibu, known as the Riviera. When all the public beaches in Malibu were closed because of COVID-19, Jeannie and I could still have some beautiful walks along the beach!

And my God will meet all your needs according to the riches of his glory in Christ Jesus.

Philippians 4:19

77.

Help for the Suffering

Jeannie and I stand on the marvelous promise in our founding Scripture. God gives us joy instead of mourning, and He inspires and strengthens us to carry out Jesus' ministry. We're grateful to the Lord for all He has done through ATG to bring comfort and hope to the suffering. Let me share some of the initiatives that have been accomplished since starting ATG.

The Poor

The first group referred to in our founding Scripture is the poor, and this is who Jesus started to minister to in His public ministry. Jeannie and I specifically asked the Lord how He wanted us to bring good news to the poverty-stricken. The day after a focused prayer session, I received a phone call from India, asking me to go and preach there. We hadn't thought about India, but as we looked up the statistics, we realized it was an obvious place to start.

Currently, 1.353 billion people live in India. The United Nations predicts it will pass China as the most populous nation by 2024. With an estimated 300 million people living on one and a half dollars or less a day, India is known as the land of the suffering. The poverty and suffering is far greater than anything we see in the West.

In going to India to preach, we wanted to help the poor as part of the trip. Getting on our knees, we prayed, "Lord, how can we best help the poor in India?" Initially, we thought about taking medical supplies. But, we soon discovered the cost and bureaucracy made it too inefficient, and so we decided there must be something else we could do.

Some friends of ours, David and Suzy Young, provided the answer. A few years earlier, Rebecca made friends with a godly man named Bradden, the son of David and Suzy. We were shocked to hear that shortly after Rebecca passed, Bradden was also called home to heaven.

David and Suzy attended Rebecca's memorial service at Holy Trinity Brompton, and after the service Suzy whispered in Jeannie's ear, "I don't think we've seen the last of each other."

David served on the board of a nonprofit organization called India Christian Ministries (ICM) that was committed to sharing the good news of Jesus in India. In 2016 we partnered with them and Reaching Indian Ministries International (RIMI) to distribute 35,000 mosquito nets and 50,000 scripture calendars in the local language. We estimate that more than 200,000 of the poorest of the poor received protection from deadly mosquito bites and God's word, telling them He loves them.

The year 2016 was one of the worst seasons for mosquitoes in recent history. The hospitals were overwhelmed and many people died. We were God's hands and feet to bring some relief to the suffering.

While I was in India, I was able to share with hundreds of pastors. After the conference, we loaded each pastor up with mosquito nets and scripture calendars to take back to their villages. It was quite a sight watching how they balanced their cargo, often on the backs of their motorbikes.

In 2018, Jeannie and I visited India and found joy in celebrating the installation of some more water wells and in praying for the villagers. We thank God that we have been able to provide clean drinking water to more than 30,000 men, women, and children in 50 villages in India. In 2021-22 we plan to reach our initial target of 100 villages.

The Brokenhearted, the Captives and the Prisoners

The brokenhearted are people who are suffering from a terrible loss. It may have been caused by the death of a loved one, the break up of a relationship or the loss of their health, finances or employment.

The captives are people who have been deeply damaged, through no fault of their own, by something that has been happened to them. For example, they may have been abused as a child.

Prisoners are people who have made bad decisions and they are now locked in darkness. For example, all addicts and people who are incarcerated.

In whatever way people are suffering, Jesus' ministry is to comfort them, restore them and empower them to turn the bad things in their lives into something good to help others. ATG is doing this.

One exciting initiative is to give messages of comfort and hope to people through social media. We are reaching millions of people around the world. More than 650,000 people follow ATG on Facebook and thousands more on other social media channels.

In every area that Satan has attacked us, we will show the victory and triumph through Jesus. Sharing comfort and hope and the treasures we have learned in the darkness. For example, there was a season when our own marriage hung by a thread. We have now produced a 20 week course called "Triumph of Marriage" which is offered in churches and available on our YouTube channel.

I have only been able to journey through all the suffering because of the life of Jesus in me (Colossians 1:27), made real to me by the Holy Spirit (John 16:4). My prayer is for you to know His victorious life in whatever you go through. Spending time with God is key to walking in His victorious life and our devotional journal app—www.atgtoday.com—carries the tag line "8 minutes that will change your life!".

After Rebecca passed, Jeannie discovered her journals. It was hard and moving for us to read these journals of Rebecca's personal walk with Jesus in the midst of all her pain and the pressures that a young person faces today. After several friends asked us to share her legacy, Jeannie wrote a devotional titled Running from the Heart, which contains excerpts from Rebecca's journals. It has inspired and encouraged people to walk with Jesus amid all the noise and suffering. The devotional is now available on the YouVersion Bible App.

Music is the food of love, and we thought it would be an effective medium to give comfort and hope to the suffering. Recently, we launched our first ATG worship song, combining the hymn "What a Friend We Have in Jesus" with the song "The Blessing." A quarter of a million people listened to the song on our YouTube channel in the first three months!

Our Partners

All the work has been undergirded by our prayer partners, a fantastic board, and many generous partners who fund the ministry—people like Fred and Lena and their extended family and friends, who have loved and supported us like family.

We have a small but brilliant team who love Jesus and want the heart of ATG to be shared to help people across the world. By God's grace, the work has been accomplished at minimum cost, and we hope, with maximum impact. Let me share with you an example of how God has provided for ATG.

One night, I had a dream about an Indian man. The next day, I had a strong sense that I should invite a man named Anand to come and work for ATG. He was the husband of Sheen, who had been doing volunteer work for our ministry. I knew nothing about their circumstances, but the day before my dream, sensing God had something else for him, Anand had handed in his notice at his job. Anand and Sheen prayed about my offer, and he came and joined us in ATG.

Anand and Sheen are talented, and it has been a pleasure to work with them in building ATG's ministry. Anand is ATG's first ministry director and he is producing the ATG songs. Jeannie and I love Anand, Sheen, and their new baby, Anna, as if they were family.

Our Vision

By God's grace, we hope to multiply ATG's work around the world. At the time of writing, there are close to 1,000 people in our five private Facebook groups (for the brokenhearted, mental health (depression and suicide prevention), addiction and marriage) and we are building a network of local churches and professionals who can help those who need extra help. Each group is led by a "Hope Warrior," someone who has turned the bad things that have happened to them into something good to help others.

Ultimately, our vision is to encourage thousands of "Hope Warriors" and to reach two billion people with the good news of Jesus Christ, one billion for Rebecca and one billion for Alex.

78.

COVID-19 and an Opportunity

As I wrote this book, the whole world went through some crazy unprecedented times. The COVID-19 pandemic turned the world upside down. No one could have imagined how people's lives would be so impacted by a virus.

With great empathy, our hearts and prayers continue to go out to the millions of people who have lost a loved one to the virus and to those who have suffered terribly during the time of isolation. Some have sunk into depression, while others have tried to escape the pain and the financial and other pressures by turning to drugs, alcohol, gambling, or porn. Still others have endured terrible loneliness.

Then there was the question of whom to blame for the pandemic. Some people, unaware of who God is and how He works, blamed God for COVID-19. Others blamed Satan. But not many asked the question, "Isn't this virus, as with all disasters that impact this planet, an indication that the world is broken and in disorder? The land needs healing. Something needs to be fixed."

One of the messages I've shared in *Living Hope* is that Jesus came to bring humankind back into relationship with God. To remove the barrier between us and Him. To satisfy God's righteous anger for our rebellion and the sins we've committed that hurt and offend Him.

The cry of my heart and my prayer, is for another great awakening to who God is and His calling on our lives. There are signs that COVID-19 and the disruption it caused has started to awaken people's hearts to Almighty God.

> *I marvel at how God works and how He is able to turn all the bad things that happen to us into something good, something of eternal value.*

In the UK, a survey by Tearfund indicated that some three million new people turned to prayer since the COVID-19 lockdown began. Whereas only five to seven percent of the nation would attend a Sunday service once a month before the virus, during the lockdown, the number jumped to 24 percent attending online church once a month. The media reported the shift in the nation and the culture. Even in the holy grail of football (soccer), several Christ-followers in the game felt emboldened to go public with their faith. Interestingly, young people have led the move toward seeking God!

During the lockdown, we noticed a threefold increase in people viewing our daily live Scripture-based video messages that include the good news of Jesus Christ. People seemed to draw closer to God, because they saw what was important in their lives.

With various distractions stripped from people's lives, and having to stay in their homes, there has been a unique opportunity to share the good news of Jesus with people who would never go to a church. I see the loving hand of our heavenly Father reaching out to touch people in the intimacy of their homes. Similar to what happened to me in 1980, we pray that the presence of God will touch people in their bedroom, in their study, in their kitchen, or wherever they are in their homes, and that they would meet the Lord Jesus Christ and be filled with His Holy Spirit.

Sensing a prompting from the Lord, we decided to produce a video, starting with my cardiac arrest and asking the question, "Why am I still alive?" We went on to tell our story with a message that God loves everyone, and just as He helped Jeannie and me in our affliction, He wants to help others too. We ended the video with the good news of Jesus Christ and an invitation for people to say what is called the sinner's prayer. Within three weeks, the video had been watched by more than 1.6 million people. The feedback was that people were struggling, many were touched and inspired, and some came to faith in Christ.

We were reminded of what Joni Eareckson Tada said, "God had permitted what He hates to accomplish what He loves!"

I experienced again that although God's heart of love is the same for every person, He reaches them in different ways.

79.

A Call to All Warriors

Through all that we have suffered, God has been working in and through Jeannie and me to give us a heart of love and empathy to turn the evil that has happened in our lives into good, to comfort and give hope to others.

We hold on to the promise in the following Scripture:

And we know that in all things God works for the good of those who love him, who have been called according to his purpose.

Romans 8:28

Through ATG, we want to encourage and inspire others to allow God to turn the bad things that have happened in their lives into something good to help others. The foundation of this message comes from this Scripture:

They will rebuild the ancient ruins, repairing cities destroyed long ago. They will revive them, though they have been deserted for many generations.

Isaiah 61:4

The question is, who are "they" in this Scripture? I believe it refers to the people God has comforted, restored, and caused to triumph that were mentioned earlier in the chapter (Isaiah 61:1)—the poor, the brokenhearted, the captives, and the prisoners!

God wants to take the people who have been crushed and broken in life and by His grace turn them into mighty warriors, people who accomplish great things to bring in God's kingdom.

Brothers and sisters, think of what you were when you were called. Not many of you were wise by human standards; not many were influential; not many were of noble birth. But God chose the foolish things of the world to shame the wise; God chose the weak things of the world to shame the strong. God chose the lowly things of this world and the despised things—and the things that are not—to nullify the things that are, so that no one may boast before him.

1 Corinthians 1:26-29

God always desires to raise up the broken to accomplish great things for His kingdom. Throughout scripture and during Jesus' ministry, God called the people the world looks down on, and He accomplished His will through them. I believe God works in this way so everyone realizes it's all about God's mercy and grace, and not about anything man has accomplished.

In the Old Testament, God raised up a shepherd boy, the youngest in his family. No one expected anything to come from his life, but God turned him into the greatest earthly king Israel ever had!

In turn, David took a group of distressed, discontented dropouts and turned them into mighty warriors. They each accomplished victory over their enemies, giving us Bible stories that have been the favorites of young boys and girls throughout history!

Warriors are people who have allowed God to comfort them, restore them, and lead them to triumph (2 Corinthians 2:14)—to take the evil that Satan caused and turn it into good for "the saving of many lives" (Genesis 50:20).

What experiences have you had that God could turn around to give comfort and hope to others?

Season Nine—The Fight of Faith

The Apostle Paul mentored a young disciple named Timothy and passed on to him the lessons he had learned in following Jesus. In his first letter to Timothy, Paul wrote:

Fight the good fight of the faith. Take hold of the eternal life to which you were called when you made your good confession in the presence of many witnesses.
1 Timothy 6:12

Nearing the end of his life, Paul wrote another letter to Timothy, and at the end of it he wrote:

I have fought the good fight, I have finished the race, I have kept the faith.
2 Timothy 4:7

Through all the suffering Paul had endured, he could say, "I have kept the faith." This was a fantastic accomplishment and something I would love to be able to say at the end of my life.

Paul had been a mighty warrior for the Lord. He had fought the fight of faith throughout his ministry, battling his flesh, the world (in the form of the religious hypocrites, Roman beatings, and angry mobs), and Satan and his demons. He is one of my biblical heroes, and I look forward to meeting him in heaven.

In this season, I share what the fight of faith is. Every follower of Christ is called to live by faith and I will share why and how faith brings victory. I've had many years in the fight of faith and I share what I have learned and some practical examples of what the fight of faith looks like.

80.

What Is the Fight of Faith?

My faith is my belief, my trust, my commitment to all that the Bible teaches about God. For example, I believe God loves me with an everlasting love and that He came to rescue me by giving His Son, Jesus Christ, to take my sin and the punishment for my sins, so that I can be forgiven and be with Him for eternity. I believe He will never abandon me. I believe God created the heavens and the earth, that He is sovereign over everything, holding every atom together by the power of His Word. Therefore, I believe He is over everything that happens in my life. If God permitted something bad to happen to me, it is part of His eternal plan and purpose.

The eternal good that will come out of my suffering will outweigh the pain of the suffering.

You may not agree with all I have just written but these are the truths that I believe, over which I fight the fight of faith.

A fight of faith occurs when thoughts or events happen that cause me to question my beliefs.

In more than forty years of following Jesus, I have had many fights regarding my faith. At times they have been hardly noticeable, like a stone in the shoe, and they were quickly resolved without changing course.

At other times, the fight has been more intense. It has stopped me on my journey until the attack was beaten off. Then there have been times when it felt as though Satan himself was trying to destroy me.

If you are a follower of Jesus Christ, you may have already had a fight of faith.

In my darkest times, everything screamed out that God had abandoned me.

The grief and pain in my heart from Alex's suicide, seeing my family so shipwrecked, experiencing Jeannie's grief-triggered hatred, and the demonic forces that constantly whispered in my ear, all shouted out that my faith in Jesus had been for nothing. My world had fallen apart.

I had an almighty fight of faith to continue to believe and hold to God's promises in the midst of my pain and suffering.

The fight of faith is to give God's Word preeminence over everything else—my feelings, my circumstances, my disappointments, and my fears. Even when I don't understand why evil has happened to me and my family, I choose to believe God's promises and to act in line with my faith. Because I trust God, this is the only thing that makes sense to me. It is a daily decision to take every thought captive and make them obedient to Christ.

The weapons we fight with are not the weapons of the world. On the contrary, they have divine power to demolish strongholds. We demolish arguments and every pretension that sets itself up against the knowledge of God, and we take captive every thought to make it obedient to Christ.

2 Corinthians 10:4-5

This, I believe, is what Jesus was referring to when He told His disciples to "deny themselves and take up their cross daily and follow me" (Luke 9:23).

The fight of faith starts in the mind. Sometimes I go many rounds with my adversary, Satan. I fight to hold to God's promises. I fight to take control of my thinking. I fight to deny my flesh. I have a choice to fight or not. In the battle, the most important thing to me is that I run as fast as I can to the throne of grace. Because it's God's grace that enables me to triumph. The life of Jesus in me, made real to me by the Holy Spirit.

> *I have learned that if I am not alert to fight and take my stand against Satan's schemes and strategy (1 Peter 5:8, 2 Corinthians 2:11, 11:3, Ephesians 6:11), I soon fall. Like Peter walking on the water, when he took his eyes off Jesus, he sank.*

81.

Why Is Faith so Important?

As a follower of Jesus Christ, I have been called to be His ambassador, to encourage and inspire people to be reconciled to God (2 Corinthians 5:20). To be an effective ambassador, I want to share with people what Jesus is like. I do this by my words and actions.

The Holy Spirit works in me to transform me into Jesus' image (Romans 8:29, Philippians 2:13). The transformation happens as I die to self and live by God's word (John 12:24, Romans 12:2).

As I fight the good fight of faith, holding to God's promises instead of letting my circumstances control me, I experience God's grace. Through God's grace, which is Jesus' life, I experience freedom and victory (John 8:31-32, 1 John 5:4, 2 Corinthians 2:14). Through the trial, my faith develops from secondhand knowledge to first hand experience of Jesus' life.

This is why the apostles Peter, Paul, and James all spoke about our suffering as something to rejoice about (Romans 5:3-5, 1 Peter 1:6-7, 4:13, James 1:2-4). Not for the suffering itself, but the opportunity it provides to become more like Christ.

In understanding why faith is so important, I can see why God works in me to develop and grow my faith, to transform me into the likeness of Jesus (Philippians 2:13, Romans 8:29, 2 Corinthians 3:18).

When everything is going well, it's easy for me to trust God and say, all things work together for good (Romans 8:28). When I face trouble and disappointment, it's not so easy to say these words, and that is when I have the opportunity to grow in my faith. In my experience, faith and pain often go together.

When the storms of life crash onto me, I'm left with a choice, to either trust that Jesus is all He says He is, or to turn away from His promises and try and find refuge elsewhere. When I choose to trust His promises, my faith grows and I discover the power of His victorious life in me.

As I mature in Christ, my faith gives me the wisdom to see and understand why God allows difficulties into my life. As hard as it is, today as I write, I still believe that God is sovereign over all that has happened to Jeannie and me. He gives me more grace to journey on, and He has developed my faith through all that I've been through, as part of His story for me.

While traveling in France, I learned that when the ground is dry in the autumn and winter, the roots of the vine have to go deep to find the water needed to survive. When this happens, the grapes are sweeter at harvest time.

> *I have learned that when I'm faced with a trial, I have an opportunity to go deeper and experience more of Jesus' amazing grace. Put another way, every bit of pain and suffering is an opportunity to experience first hand the victorious life of Christ.*

82.

How Do I Fight the Fight of Faith?

When I feel crushed by the waves of grief and pain, I need an anchor for my soul, something that will keep me from being washed away from my faith in Christ. My anchor has three parts to it.

Love

The fight of faith takes place in the mind, but it's decided in the heart.

Love is the most powerful thing in the universe, and God's love is poured into my heart by the Holy Spirit:

And hope does not put us to shame, because God's love has been poured out into our hearts through the Holy Spirit, who has been given to us.

Romans 5:5

Over the years, God's love has been poured into my heart again and again, and my love for Jesus Christ has grown deeper and deeper.

My love for God is stronger than life itself. I would rather die than hurt or offend Him. His love is my motivation to lay my life down for Him.

For Christ's love compels us, because we are convinced that one died for all, and therefore all died. And he died for all, that those who live should no longer live for themselves but for him who died for them and was raised again.

2 Corinthians 5:14-15

When the fight of faith raged over what had happened to my family and me, I had already decided in my heart that I could never abandon the lover of my soul!

Questions and doubts still came to my mind, but my course was settled in my heart.

As Job said, "Though He slay me, yet will I trust Him" (Job 13:15).

I have learned the importance of keeping my heart in God's love, as one of my favorite Scriptures says,

Above all else, guard your heart, for everything you do flows from it.

Proverbs 4:23

My faith and love for God is shown by how I live and what I think and do. As Jesus said,

Whoever has my commands and keeps them is the one who loves me. The one who loves me will be loved by my Father, and I too will love them and show myself to them.

John 14:21

Scripture Memorization

After my encounter with God in 1980, the Bible came alive to me. It was food for my hungry soul, and I devoured it day and night. I developed a habit of memorizing up to 10 Scriptures, taken from the devotional Daily Light, in the morning and meditating on the words whenever I had some free time in the day.

After Alex passed, someone sent me a postcard every day for a year with the word "Love" on one side and a Scripture on the other. To this day, I don't know who sent me the cards, but I still take some of them each day, memorize them, and carry them with me in my heart. Jeannie and I have a joke that if I can correctly repeat them, she gives me a gold star.

I love what the psalmist wrote:

> *How can a young person stay on the path of purity? By living according to your word. I have hidden your word in my heart that I might not sin against you.*
>
> **Psalm 119:10-11**

I have hidden God's Word in my heart, and I'm ready for the Holy Spirit to remind me of the right scriptures, when my adversary speaks lies into my mind.

For example, one of the attacks on my faith, a lie that Satan spoke into my mind in my affliction, was that I should run from God. I thought, where could I go? I considered the options and quickly decided that God had me hemmed in. Wherever I went, He would be there. I felt like the psalmist, who said,

If I go up to the heavens, you are there; if I make my bed in the depths, you are there. If I rise on the wings of the dawn, if I settle on the far side of the sea, even there your hand will guide me, your right hand will hold me fast.

Psalm 139:8-10

Satan knows that as long as I have faith in God's Word, he can't touch me. The only hope he has of stopping me on my mission, my purpose, is by moving me away from standing on God's Word. He does this in the same way he deceived Eve in the garden of Eden, by getting me to believe a lie.

Discouragement and disappointment are the softening up process before a direct attack on my faith. That's why I need to brush them off quickly by giving them over to the Lord (Matthew 10:14, 1 Peter 5:7). If I don't, I start to question whether God was with me in the past, and then it becomes very hard to trust Him for the present and the for future.

I have learned the power of God's Word as an anchor for my soul.

The Holy Spirit

The Holy Spirit gives me the divine understanding of God's grace, teaching me about the life of Jesus in me. Part of that life is perseverance, the ability to keep going when everything is screaming at me to give up. In holding to God's promises, I received the three epiphanies I mentioned in Season Seven. The truth in those epiphanies helped to set me free from the crushing weight of my pain and suffering. As Jesus said to His followers,

If you hold to my teaching, you are really my disciples. Then you will know the truth, and the truth will set you free.

John 8:31-32

I have learned that:

- the Holy Spirit comforts, helps, pours in more love, empowers, and reveals Jesus' life to me;

- to live by faith is:

> *• the currency of earth and the treasure in heaven, and;*

> *• to conduct one's life in the certain knowledge that God is real and all His promises are true and can be trusted;*

- with my shield of faith, I can extinguish the lies that Satan throws into my mind. I resist the lies with the truth of God's Word;

- to have peace in the storm, exercising my faith to trust that God is with me and He will carry me through;

- when things don't work out as I want, my faith allows me to trust and believe that God is working a bigger eternal plan through my situation; and

- by faith I should never, ever, ever give up.

83.

Examples of the Fight of Faith

I've shared my understanding of what scripture teaches about the "Fight of Faith," but what did this look like in practice? In sharing some of the practical fights of faith I have had in the last few years, I pray that you will be inspired and encouraged when the storms of life break over your life and you are left with a choice of either holding to God's promises or taking things into your own hands.

Taking Offense

Jeannie and I had reason to take offense at God for all the evil things that had happened in our lives.

We had surrendered our lives to God's will, leaving behind our goals and dreams and serving Him in London. Giving away our possessions and starting with little or no money, we trusted God and built our lives on His promises. In line with His promises, God mightily blessed our family, our work, our ministry, and our finances. It had been a season of great prosperity and fruit.

And then our world fell apart, and I found myself being tempted to take offense at God. After all that God had done through us, how could

He have allowed Alex to commit suicide? In her grief, Jeannie couldn't reconcile how a loving God could allow Alex to die in such an untimely, painful, lonely, and evil way, and she lost her faith for two years or so.

Maybe you have taken offense with God because of something that has happened in your life. If so, we understand, and we want you to know that God is not mad at you. The truth is that suffering is one of the main reasons that people lose their faith, and it's one of the main barriers that keeps people from coming to faith in Christ.

God, in His great mercy, rescued me from this particular attack on my faith, and He opened my eyes to His warning in Scripture as follows.

John the Baptist was used powerfully by God. After spending most of his life in the open air, with the freedom to announce the kingdom of God, he was locked up in a small, dark, smelly prison cell. We know he was struggling because, although he had seen and already recognized his cousin Jesus as the Messiah, in prison, he started to question who He was (Matthew 11:3).

Judging by Jesus' response, "blessed is he who does not take offense at me," it appears that John the Baptist was struggling in his faith. He was probably starting to think, "I hate it in this prison cell; why hasn't Jesus rescued me?" And he started to question whether Jesus was the Messiah.

Earlier, Jesus had told His disciples they needed to eat His flesh and drink His blood if they wanted to be His disciples (John 6:54, 56). In other words, to genuinely follow Him, they had to lay down their lives and be a living sacrifice (Romans 12:1). It was a high calling, and Jesus asked them, "Does this offend you?" (John 6:61). Many disciples turned away from Jesus when they realized the cost (John 6:66), but the twelve stayed.

I believe Jesus particularly warned against taking offense at Him because He knew how Satan would attack us in this way.

Self-Pity

Similar to having reason for taking offense, I have also had a fight of faith to keep my eyes on Jesus and His eternal purpose for my life, and not to focus on all the things that have been taken from me.

> *I have learned that if I take my eyes off Jesus, I quickly start to sink into the waves of despair and self-pity that are ready to overwhelm my life.*

These are some of the areas that I have had to surrender to God and how I have switched my thinking and attitude from being negative to being loving and positive.

Every day, Jeannie and I miss our children, Rebecca and Alex. And, for years while living in the U.S., we have also missed Ben, because he was living in the UK.

We missed being with them, and we missed all that Rebecca and Alex could have been. I would have loved to have seen our prayers answered as they grew in their relationship with the Lord. I would have loved to have walked Rebecca down the aisle, watched Alex reach his potential in athletics, dote and pray over the grandchildren, and see our family grow.

It was not that long after Rebecca went home to heaven that some friends invited us to join them at their church in Chicago. At the start of the service, the pastor's wife shared a story of thanksgiving. Their daughter had walked away from the Lord and had made many mistakes. But she had come back to the Lord and had married a wonderful Christian man. That morning, the pastor's wife had heard that her daughter had given birth to their first grandchild, and she asked us all to stand and sing "Great Is Thy Faithfulness."

Jeannie and I looked at each other, hugged, held hands, and with tears pouring down our faces, we sang "Great is thy faithfulness." That morning, it was a real sacrifice to give thanks and praise to God. I believe the Lord saw our hearts as we chose to thank and praise Him (Psalm 50:23).

My brother and his wife have six children and fourteen grandchildren. Of course, Satan attacks us by saying God has been unkind to us, and we've lost out. We defeat the attack by thanking God for His blessing on my brother's family and asking Him to bless them even more. We thank God for the time we had with Rebecca, Ben, and Alex and for the inheritance that is waiting for us in heaven (1 Peter 1:3-4).

One of my friends who worked for me in HSBC reached a senior position in the bank. Recently, he retired on a fantastic pension, and is enjoying a well-earned retirement. Satan whispers to me that I missed out by following Jesus. I defeat the attack by thanking God for His blessing on my friend and by choosing to be grateful for His marvelous grace for me today and the eternal rewards that await me in heaven.

In every fight of faith, we refuse to yield to the attack, and instead, we hold on to God's promises. Jesus is the Lord of our lives and He has a specific work for us to do.

We can never lose out in God's economy and plan, and as Jesus promised, whatever He has asked us to surrender to Him He makes up one hundredfold in this life and through eternity (Mark 10:29-30).

Patience

To encourage His disciples to pray and never to give up, Jesus told His disciples a parable about a widow. The widow was crying out to an unjust judge for justice against her adversary. Because of her persistence, the unjust judge decided to give her justice. The message of the parable is, if an unjust judge answers the persistent cries of a widow, how much more will God quickly give justice to His children (Luke 18:1-8).

Scripture teaches that God will give me justice against my adversary, Satan, for all the evil that has happened to me.

When we moved to Malibu, doors were opening, and my hope to see God turn the evil and tragedy in my life into something good, seemed near at hand. We were about to see the Lord glorified through all that had happened.

After the initial flurry of interest and activity, everything settled down. We were thankful for the fruit we did see from our ATG ministry, but in my mind, it was not commensurate with the suffering we had gone through. Jeannie also struggled with this fight of faith. She said, "We had greater impact for the kingdom of God when you served Him in London and when you were running Alpha USA. What has been the point of all our pain and suffering?"

Charles Spurgeon said the greatest test of faith is "non-success." I was having a mighty fight of faith to trust that God had not abandoned us and that He would fulfill the promises in His Word—for example, "to crush Satan under our feet" (Romans 16:20) and "to quickly give us justice against our adversary" (Luke 18:8).

y real struggle was in the fact that in the story of the persistent widow, Jesus had said the Father would give justice quickly, but time seemed to be passing painfully slowly.

Once again, the Holy Spirit came to my rescue, and I was encouraged by the stories in the Bible.

Joseph had to wait 13 years as a slave and in prison before God promoted him to be prime minister of one of the most powerful nations in the world.

David had to wait approximately 13 years in exile in the wilderness before he became king.

Jesus had 30 years without any public ministry. Just imagine how many people He could have healed and set free if He had started His public ministry at 13 instead of 30! When He did start His public ministry, His father said at His baptism,

This is my Son, whom I love; with Him I am well pleased.
Matthew 3:17

The fact that Jesus waited so long before His public ministry is, I believe, a clear message that we are called to minister before God and the angelic beings, as well as before others.

God's purpose in all this was to use the church to display His wisdom in its rich variety to all the unseen rulers and authorities in the heavenly places.
Ephesians 3:10 (NLT)

It's awesome to think of the privilege we have to display God's wisdom and purpose to the angelic beings by how we live out the good news of Jesus. For the angels, it must be mind-blowing to see how God can display His glory through such weak beings as humans. And that is the point; God's glory is seen in our weakness.

In a season when I was struggling with "non-success," the Lord whispered into my ear, "You are the boast of heaven!" It brought tears to my eyes, and Jeannie wept when I told her what God had said to me.

The Lord's thoughts and ways are so much higher than ours (Isaiah 55:8-9). He sees our faithfulness, and I believe it pleases Him.

John Bunyan, who wrote The Pilgrim's Progress, said, "A man when he suffers for Christ is set upon a hill, upon a stage as in a theatre, to play a part for God in the world."

Are you struggling with non-success, with the thought that you're not doing anything meaningful for the Lord? If so, I pray you will be inspired and encouraged by what I learned about being patient.

I learned that God doesn't value the same things we do, and patiently waiting for His timing is essential to fulfill His purpose for my life.

> *I have learned that:*
>
> *- I must hold to a simple trust in Jesus Christ to fulfill His promises at just the right time;*
>
> *- when God is silent, I need to cling to His promises and trust Him to fulfill them; and*
>
> *- fighting the good fight of faith in everyday living, when there is no tangible success, is of great worth in God's eyes and will make you the "boast of heaven."*

Keep being faithful and don't ever give up. Your appointment is waiting for you. Don't get discouraged or disappointed, because your abundant blessings are about to come through! Stay consistent and don't despise the day of small things (Zechariah 4:10).

Take heart because, at just the right time, God will suddenly promote you to your public service to Him.

So, let's not get tired of doing what is good. At just the right time we will reap a harvest of blessing if we don't give up.

Galatians 6:9 (NLT)

84.

Wrestling with God

One of the unusual stories in the Old Testament is of Jacob wrestling all night with an angel (Genesis 32:24-28). Jacob refused to let the angel go unless He blessed him. In the final exchange, the angel told Jacob that his name was being changed from Jacob (meaning self rules) to Israel (God rules), "because you have struggled with God and with humans and have overcome."

Some scholars believe the angel was actually Jesus before His incarnation. Clearly, there is a powerful message in this story.

This was the turning point in Jacob's life, the point when he started to fulfill his purpose.

I believe there are times when God takes us to a deep place with Him, and as with Jacob, He wants us to wrestle in prayer, to bring in His kingdom on earth. These Scriptures support this view:

And from the days of John the Baptist until now the kingdom of heaven suffers violence, and the violent take it by force.
Matthew 11:12 (NKJV)

The people who know their God
will be strong and carry out great exploits.
Daniel 11:32 (NKJV)

There are times when God calls us to pray and not give up, to remind Him of His promises until He brings in His kingdom.

I have set watchmen upon your walls, O Jerusalem, who will never hold their peace day or night; you who are His servants and by your prayers put the Lord in remembrance of His promises, keep not silence, and give Him no rest until He establishes Jerusalem and makes her a praise in the earth.

Isaiah 62:6, 7 (AMP)

Shortly before finishing *Living Hope*, a great burden came upon me for God to fulfill His will and purpose in our lives. I wrote down several Scriptures speaking of God's desire to answer our prayers and bring in His kingdom on earth.

I didn't believe God had permitted Alex's suicide and Rebecca's passing for no reason! It didn't line up with scripture. I believed with all my heart that God was going to turn the evil that had happened to us into something good to bring glory to His name.

Scripture is clear that we should pray and expect God to turn any evil and tragedy in our lives into something good for His glory and kingdom. Jesus finishes the parable of the persistent widow with the words, "However, when the Son of Man comes will He find faith on the earth?"

I sensed God was laying a burden on my heart to pray and not to give up until God gave me justice against my adversary. I needed to wrestle in prayer to enter a season of intercession.

85.

Intercession

In my time of wrestling with God, my prayers became more intense. I would get up in the middle of the night in our small apartment, get down on my knees, and pray from the bottom of my heart. Deep sobbing would rise up from within, and I would quote God's promises at Him. Sometimes I would get angry and shout out to God that He had to fulfill His promises.

"Lord, You must fulfill Your Word," I would cry. "We can't go through eternity without Your Word being fulfilled." Satan would whisper in my ear, "Oh, these Scriptures don't apply to your situation." But I refused to accept his lies.

I had many Scriptures that I would pray again and again. For example:

So, don't you think God will surely give justice to His chosen people who cry out to Him day and night? Will He keep putting them off? I tell you, He will grant justice to them quickly!

Luke 18:7-8 (NLT)

I will repay you for the years the locusts have eaten.

Joel 2:25

Those who hope in me will not be disappointed.
Isaiah 49:23

I would call out to God to answer my prayers and to reveal His glory through our brokenness. I would pray,

"Lord, Moses would not accept anyone (the angel of the Lord), it had to be You—How will anyone know that we are Your people unless You go with us? **This is about Your glory, the fulfillment of Your Word!**

Daniel knew Your Word and could see the seventy-year captivity was coming to an end. So He set His face to seek God and see His will fulfilled. **This is about Your glory, the fulfillment of Your Word!**

Nehemiah was deeply troubled by the state of Jerusalem because he knew this was not how it was supposed to be. He set about making it right. **This is about Your glory, the fulfillment of Your Word!**

David was deeply offended by how Goliath was speaking to the children of Israel and decided to fight him. **This is about Your glory, the fulfillment of Your Word!**

Gideon had mighty power because he knew that what was happening to the children of Israel was not right. It was out of line with Your love and character and Your Word. **This is about Your glory, the fulfillment of Your Word!**

Oh, Lord, fulfill Your Word, make good Your covenant with me in Jesus Christ!"

After a couple of hours, I'd go back to bed exhausted.

Finally, after months of interceding on my knees, the Lord's peace came upon me. It was a beautiful morning, and we had the screen open toward the ocean. I felt the sun on my face, and I could smell the fresh salty air from the crashing waves. As clear as a whistle, God spoke to me. He said, "Gerard, trust me. I will fulfill My Word at the right time."

In those few words, I knew my prayers were answered. In His time we will see His glory shining through all that He has allowed to happen to us. Overwhelming triumph is ours because of Jesus' victory on the cross. He has given us a living hope, moment by moment and day by day.

A few days after the Lord spoke to me, I was enjoying a peaceful walk with Chloe on the beach, and the Lord told me to read the commentary of one of my favorite authors, Charles Spurgeon, on Psalm 28. Psalm 28:1 says:

> *Unto thee will I cry, O Lord, my rock. Be not silent to me.*

Straightaway the psalmist's words seemed to resonate with how I had been praying. And then I read Charles Spurgeon's commentary:

> When God seems to close his ear, we must not therefore close our mouths, but rather cry with more earnestness; for when our note grows shrill with eagerness and grief, he will not long deny us a hearing. What a dreadful case should we be in if the Lord should become forever silent to our prayers! This thought suggested itself to David, and he turned it into a plea, thus teaching us to argue and reason with God in our prayers.

A few days later I was reading Psalm 31, and the first verse broke over me like a wave on the beach, reminding me of how I had cried out to God:

> *Let me never be ashamed.*

When I read Charles Spurgeon's commentary, my heart leaped within me:

> How can the Lord permit the man to be ultimately put to shame who depends alone upon Him? This would not be dealing like a God of truth and grace. It would bring dishonour upon God Himself if faith were not in the end rewarded. It will be an ill day indeed for religion when trust in God brings no consolation and no assistance.

> *I have learned that sometimes God lays a great burden upon us to pray in His kingdom and purposes. God wants us to remind Him of His promises. And, knowing the matter is settled in heaven, God's peace will give rest to my soul, and I can trust Him to answer my prayers in His perfect time.*

86.

Be in the Moment

An important part of our fight of faith is trusting God each day. Trust Him that you are where He wants you to be, and when it is time to move, He is quite able to tell you!

Shortly after my season of intercession, of specifically praying for God's promises to be fulfilled in my life, the Lord spoke to me and said, "Gerard, be in the moment." For several months I had been carrying a heavenly burden to pray in God's kingdom, for His will to be done on earth, but now He wanted me to have a season of being still and to enjoy Him.

Having received peace in the certain knowledge that my intercessory prayers would be answered, God wanted me to enjoy every moment with Him.

I'm learning to not be robbed of each moment God has given me on earth. Be in the moment.

How easy it is to become weary with activity. Instead, enjoy the journey and consider what God has put into your hand. Take a moment to be inspired by a sunrise, to savor the delicious food you eat and the clean water you drink, pause to smell the jasmine and honeysuckle, listen to the birds singing, and thank God for the moon and the stars.

Be thankful and make the most of every moment you have with your spouse, children, and loved ones. I miss Rebecca and Alex, and I'm grateful for the times I had with them when they were still with us!

The special moments in life need to be recognized and appreciated, and not wasted by wishing for something else.

This is the day the Lord has made; we will rejoice and be glad in it.

Psalm 118:24

I have learned that I bring God glory when I believe He has me where He wants me, in my marriage, my home and location, my work, and even the small details of life.

I'm learning to be in the moment!

What about You?

One of my prayers in writing this book is that you will awaken to God's great love for you and His purpose for your life. My prayer, with every breath and heartbeat, is that you will see how God wants to turn anything bad or evil in your life into something good to help you and others.

Whatever you may have experienced in your life, I hope you can see and be encouraged by the hand of the master weaver. Be grateful for the golden threads, and by God's grace, for the dark ones too. Your purpose is your life beautifully weaved together as a tapestry for God's glory—the revelation of Jesus Christ—in loving, sharing and serving others!

One of my favorite movies is Schindler's List. I love the end of the movie. The war is over, and Schindler realizes he could have done more to save the Jews. He breaks down and crys. He had done well, but he could have done more!

As an athlete, I never wanted to finish a race and think, "I had more to give. I could have done better!"

Like Jeannie and me, I'm sure that you don't want to finish life and think, "I could have done more for Jesus." Paul said, "I have finished my race, I kept the faith." He had no regrets!

All that God asks of you is to complete the work that has been assigned to you, which is your purpose. In doing that, you bring glory to His name. And that is worth living for.

> *I have brought you glory on earth by finishing
> the work you gave me to do.*

John 17:4

As I look back over my life I can see the hand of the master weaver working to bring me to my purpose. From my roots, the years at military school, my athletics, meeting Jeannie, family, church and work, the tests of faith, all the good times and even the years of suffering, were all golden, multicolor, and dark threads weaved together as a tapestry, as part of God's eternal story and for His glory!

Nothing is a coincidence in God's kingdom. It's perfectly designed for His divine plan and purpose.

> *Your eyes saw my unformed body; all the days ordained for me were
> written in your book before one of them came to be.*

Psalm 139:16

Perhaps in reading *Living Hope* you realize you know about God, but now you would like to receive His forgiveness and invite Him to be Lord of your life. If so, please pray this simple prayer:

Lord Jesus Christ, I'm sorry for the things I have done to hurt and offend You and others.

Thank You for dying on the cross for me so that I can be forgiven and for giving me eternal life.

Please come into my heart and be Lord of my life. I want to welcome the

Holy Spirit into my heart, and with His help, I want to live the rest of my life to please You. Amen.

By God's grace and your faith, may you enjoy your walk with Jesus, the lover of your soul. May you have a living hope and enter fully into a victorious life for Him, and may He fill you with the knowledge of His divine purpose for your life.

And now, may the Lord bless you and be gracious unto you, and give you His peace. May your faith be awakened and may you journey on with peace in your heart in the certain knowledge that you are loved by Almighty God and that He has an eternal purpose for your life.

It seems right to me that I should end *Living Hope* with three of my favorite Scriptures.

*Praise be to the God and Father of our Lord Jesus Christ! In his great mercy he has given us new birth into a **living hope** through the resurrection of Jesus Christ from the dead, and into an inheritance that can never perish, spoil or fade. This inheritance is kept in heaven for you, who through faith are shielded by God's power until the coming of the salvation that is ready to be revealed in the last time.*

1 Peter 1:3-5

The best—no, the *very best*—is yet to come

Acknowledgements

Living Hope is my story about my journey thus far, and I've had the privilege and joy to make friends with many remarkable people. They have loved, supported, and prayed for me and without them I would not have made it! I now have an opportunity to thank you and I have listed many names. If I've missed your name, please forgive me.

Jeannie, my soul mate, my other half, my wife of over forty years, thank you. We have journeyed together over mountain tops and deep dark valleys and my love for you today is deeper than it's ever been.

Ben, my son, thank you for your love and courage. You have journeyed through so many heart-breaking storms and you have never given up. I love you and I'm so proud of you.

To dear friends who have gone the second and third mile to love, support, open your homes and pray for Jeannie and me, thank you. Jami and Bill Voge, George and Judy Kohl, Nigel and Sally Wolven, Mark and Jenny Emery, Fred and Lena Koury, Kris and Kimby Gray, David and Tina Segel, Susan and Mark Neaman, Nick and Jo West, Robert and Ros Norton, Laura and Kosta Georgakakos and Lani Netter.

To my family, and especially my brother Kim and his wife Jackie, my mother-in-law Marion Anderson and my brother-in-law Austin Anderson, thank you for your love, support and prayers.

To my extraordinary friends who helped to save my life on that fateful night, what can I say! Deryck and Rozie Van Rensburg and sons Joel and Josiah and my special friend Adam Anschultz, thank you. Without you I would literally not be here today. Together with our friends Jonathan and Hannah Beck, thank you for going the second mile in praying and caring for Jeannie and me in the hours and days after my cardiac arrest.

To the first responders from Station 71, led so well by Chad, thank you. You saved my life.

Deepest gratitude to my fantastic medical team at UCLA hospital and especially my cardiologist Dr. Mazar and my electrophysiologist Dr. Macias.

To my friends and co-laborers in Awakening to God Ministries (ATG), it's an honor and a privilege to serve with you. Thank you for your love and prayers and for all your wonderful work to help spread the message of God's love around the globe. Anand and Sheen Paul, you are like a son and daughter to Jeannie and me and we love you and baby Anna so much. Loya Dutta, Abraham Balat and intern Natalie Hardt, thank you for your hard work and support. Mike Berry and Marianna Gergel, thank you for your help with all the financial accounting for ATG.

To those who kindly endorsed *Living Hope*, thank you, I am very grateful.

To our friends and prayer partners, without your love, encouragement and support we would not have made it. Daniel and Elissa Strumphler, Tim and Mary Funk, Burt and Angelika Louhof Giada, Bob and Wendy Wolff, Lee and Gretchen Koury, Kevin and Marilyn Malone, Jill and Scott Carter, Kim Gates, Brian and Page Weissmann, Tyler and Christy Lennon, John and Stephanie Davis, Laura Landoe, Marjorie Gearhart, Will and Nancy Carnes, Dave and Lachele Kawala,

Mike and Penny Campbell, Todd and Carolyn Burns, Marc and Julie Davies, James Hussney, Stan and Jennifer Janowiak, Ike and Christine Hong, David and Misty Grieger, Louanne Felzan, Ed and Dawn DeDomenico, Tom and Jan Rowe, Paul and Barbara Hickman, Bob and Vicky Souster, Alan and Phillipa Green, Sally Hawkins, Mike and Cherie Singh, Mike and Christy Changaris, Ray Carter, Jon and Anna Burton, Ted Harms, Phil and Nancy Anschutz, Bridget and Todd Baumgartner, Ted and Lili Baehr, Jessie and Tyler Friedi, June and Jim Sharman, Marceline and Jonathan Delaureal, DeeAnn Freeman, John and Dolores Jazwa, Jim and Ginny Roodhouse, Kathy Sparrenberger, Elaine Sweas, Andrea Symons, Bob and Cathy Tate, Jammie Treadwell, John and Hiroko Wilson, Maggie and Reinier Pranger, George Kohl III, Bill and Stefanie Fisher, William and Kathleen Mudd, Bill and Cindy Bell Parsley, Steve and Mary Rose Zoller, Judy and Scott Gration, Lori Glattly, Rick and Jeannie Anderson, Jonathan and Susan Dick, Kay Horner, Bradley Stuart, Nick and Bonnie Fletcher, Jeriel Sunand, Max and Alex Brady, Andy and Linda Morris, Pati Boddy, Bill and Theresa Armour, Steve and Joanie Alley, Scott and Jackie Renwick, Bernard and Connie St Louis, Paul and Patti Tyska, Eddie and Diana Nassar, Bill Abington, David and Karen Thomas, Jerry and Julie Bott, David and Lisa Brown, Sharon and Ralph Leavitt, Lenny and Penny Decanay, Meisha Johnson, Brad and Glad Bradshaw, Scott and Peggie Kaase, Tom Woods, Gunnel Larsson, Madeline Voge, Mary Cade, Pat Denson, Sharon Anderson, John Barrington, Charles Mclaren, and John and Leigh McNairy.

To our wonderful Hope Warriors, thank you for your courage and for pioneering the work to turn every bit of pain into something good to help others. Julie Davies, Laura Georgakakos, Jack Kehoe and Frank Gatera.

Many thanks to the Malibu Men's Prayer group that has encouraged and inspired me over the last five years. Kris Gray, Bob Wolff, Jonathan Morris, Jake Herbert, Marc Davies, Stephen Polk, Michael Thomas,

Ken Blanchard, Richard Scott, Adam Anschultz, Stan Janowiak, Max Adams, Adam McCants and many others.

To my wonderful church family in the U.S., UK and around the world, a huge thank you. You have loved, supported and prayed for Jeannie and me over the years and we would not have made it without you. Nick and Jo West and the saints at New Life Church, London, Nicky and Pippa Gumbel and the saints at HTB, London, and the Alpha family around the world, Ger Jones and Ron Cross and the saints at Vintage Church in Santa Monica and Malibu, Los Angeles (Ger, thank you for coming to see and pray for me after my cardiac arrest), Mike Woodruff and the saints at Christ Church, Lake Forest, the saints in the wonderful house church that met at George and Judy's home in Lake Forest, Illinois, Jonathan Schaeffer and the saints at Grace Church, Middleburg Heights, Ohio, Scott Chapman and the saints at The Chapel, Illinois, Steve Murray and the saints at La Jolla Community Church, Los Angeles, Simon Downing and the saints at Aldwick Baptist Church, UK, Martin and Viv French and Benjamin John and the saints at Kings Gate Church, Bognor Regis, UK.

My gratitude goes to my new friend Geoffrey Berwin, my writing coach Sarah Brown and the rest of the Steve Harrison publishing team who gave me excellent advice and encouragement in writing and promoting Living Hope. Many thanks to my copy editor Marcia Ford and the editors and first readers who gave excellent feedback. E. Catherine Lappe, Christine Gershom, Neeta Manohar, Natalie Hardt, Todd Burns, Nigel Wolven, Jami Voge and George Kohl. I am grateful for all the encouragement and prayers I received from so many of my friends throughout the writing of Living Hope. Most of all, I want to thank my darling Jeannie for all that you added to Living Hope as we read and reread the manuscript many times, and for your patience and endurance as we carried this project while moving across the pond!

To my friends at Integrity Financial, thank you for letting me share your office space allowing me some quiet writing time in the evenings. Kris Gray, Lockwood Holmes Jr., Chris Riboli, Adam Anschultz and Jeremey Cumbee.

To our friends and partners at India Christian Ministries, thank you, it's an honor and a privilege to serve with you.

To my tennis buddies who provided so many fun times during my stay in Malibu, thank you. Michael Rubin, Rey Cano, Christine Burton, Debbie Becker, Steve, Gary Bowen, Peter Sinding.

*For more photos and memories, please visit: **livinghopebook.com***

M I N I S T R I E S

Living Hope is a resource of Awakening to God Ministries.

All profits from Living Hope will go to help the suffering via Awakening to God Ministries.

The mission of ATG Ministries is to provide love, comfort and hope to people in the US and around the world who are suffering.

Learn more at:
www.awakeningtogod.org

***

Other resources by Gerard and Jeannie Long are available at:
store.awakeningtogod.org

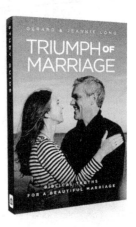

Follow us on social media:

 awakeningtogod   awakeningtogod    awakeningtogod   atg_ministries

Made in the USA
Columbia, SC
24 February 2022